Eagle
Seamanship

Eagle
Seamanship
A Manual for Square-Rigger Sailing

FOURTH EDITION

Revised by
CAPT Eric C. Jones, USCG, and
LT Christopher D. Nolan, USCG

Naval Institute Press
Annapolis, Maryland

Naval Institute Press
291 Wood Road
Annapolis, MD 21402

Cover image: *Eagle* under full sail, c. 1953

Library of Congress Cataloging-in-Publication Data
Eagle seamanship : a manual for square-rigger sailing. — 4th ed. / rev.
by Eric C. Jones and Christopher D. Nolan.
     p. cm.
  Includes index.
  ISBN 978-1-59114-631-5 (pbk. : alk. paper) 1. Seamanship—Handbooks,
manuals, etc. 2. Sailing—Handbooks, manuals, etc. 3. United States.
Coast Guard—Officers' handbooks. 4.   Eagle (Ship)—Handbooks,
manuals, etc. I. Jones, Eric C., date II. Nolan, Christopher D., date
  VK541.E34 2011
  623.88'226—dc22

                         2010043937

Printed in the United States of America on acid-free paper

14 13 12 11   9 8 7 6 5 4 3 2 1
First printing

CONTENTS

ILLUSTRATIONS

FOREWORD

This manual has been in existence in one form or another since the late 1940s; it is a working document. The information contained in the manual has been refined over the decades by *Eagle*'s officers and crews, and used by generations of U.S. Coast Guard Academy cadets during their training cruises in *Eagle*. Because *Eagle Seamanship* is based on long-standing traditions of working a square-rigger, and sized to be easily carried in the pocket, it may be used by all hands that sail in *Eagle* as well as sailors of other square-rigged vessels.

A commissioned U.S. Coast Guard cutter, the barque-rigged sailing ship *Eagle* is an ideal platform to train cadets and officer candidates in seamanship and navigation, while also engendering the leadership skills required for them to develop into proficient seagoing watch officers.

Since the trainees in *Eagle* are involved in all aspects of the operation of this Coast Guard cutter, this manual assists senior cadets to hone and carry out leadership skills, while junior cadets and officer candidates learn their duties and carry out followership skills through "working the ship."

This new edition of *Eagle Seamanship* is concise, informative, and instructive for cadets, officer candidates, and others who will use it for their personal development in becoming U.S. Coast Guard officers and square-rigger sailors.

I served in *Eagle* for twelve of my thirty-three years in the U.S. Coast Guard and often reflect on the many experiences I had that helped to develop my skills as a professional mariner. While challenging at times, sailing a square-rigger and training others has provided some of my fondest memories. If you have the chance to sail in *Eagle* I trust you'll find it just as rewarding, and to all who use this manual I wish you "Fair winds and royals all the way!"

CWO4 (BOSN) RICHARD T. "RED" SHANNON, USCG (RET.)
Sailing on board in the North Atlantic Ocean with OCS Class 10-02
March 2010

ACKNOWLEDGMENTS

*E*agle Seamanship was originally edited by William I. Norton, USCGR, and published in 1969. It was later revised by CAPT Paul M. Regan, USCG, in 1976 and was published by Naval Institute Press that same year. The insights of then commanding officer RADM Paul A. Welling and sailing master CWO4 Richard T. "Red" Shannon played an important part in that edition. The history section was originally written by Robert Dixon Jr., and was later revised and updated by Paul H. Johnson, head librarian, U.S. Coast Guard Academy. The third edition, published by Naval Institute Press in 1990, came about due to the work of CAPT (then LT) Edwin H. Daniels Jr., CAPT Ernst M. Cummings (*Eagle*'s eighteenth commanding officer), CAPT David T. Wood (*Eagle*'s nineteenth commanding officer) and CAPT (then CDR) Robert F. Petko.

For this fourth edition, in addition to the aforementioned contributors, the authors would like to thank especially ADM Robert J. Papp Jr. (*Eagle*'s twenty-second commanding officer and current Coast Guard commandant), RADM Patrick M. Stillman (*Eagle*'s twentieth commanding officer), CAPT Ivan T. Luke Jr. (*Eagle*'s twenty-third commanding officer), and CAPT J. Christopher Sinnett (*Eagle*'s twenty-fifth commanding officer), for imparting copious amounts of *Eagle* wisdom upon us.

Finally, special thanks to the Naval Institute Press staff, and in particular Thomas J. Cutler, for helping bring *Eagle Seamanship* into the twenty-first century.

Eagle has been, and sailing remains, one of the most fundamental and tangible experiences a future mariner will ever have. As the common seagoing experience for nearly all active Coast Guard officers, *Eagle*'s value to the Coast Guard and the nation cannot be overstated. It is in her engine room, on her decks, and in her rig that our future maritime leaders, guardians, and policy makers get their first taste of the nation's oldest continuous seagoing service and its importance to the nation. Despite being nearly seventy-five years old and a century removed from the Age of Sail, *Eagle*'s mission remains valid, her experiences remain authentic, and her crew and trainees remain committed to the Coast Guard's motto of *Semper Paratus*.

Eagle
Seamanship

CHAPTER 1

Eagle History

Today's square-rigged barque *Eagle* is the seventh Coast Guard vessel to bear that name. The *Eagles* span many years and many changes.

The Coast Guard traces its history to ten revenue cutters authorized by the first Congress in 1790 at the instigation of Alexander Hamilton, the first secretary of the treasury. These ten cutters (so called for their English rig) operated as the Revenue Marine in collecting customs duties and enforcing the revenue laws.

The first *Eagle* was stationed in Savannah, Georgia, under the command of Capt. John Howell. Howell's *Eagle* served as the Georgia cutter from 1792 until 1798 or 1799, when she was replaced by a captured French vessel and renamed *Bee*. The United States had entered into an undeclared naval war with France in 1796. This war with the nation's former ally intensified when some sixty to eighty French privateers based at Guadeloupe in the West Indies continued to molest American ships. In May 1798 the United States Navy was formed to meet such threats and hastily acquired fifty-four vessels, of which eight were revenue cutters. This cooperation with the new navy established a custom that has been observed in all wars down through the years and remains in practice today.

The war with France was a strange war for it depended on sailing skill and bluff as much as on gunfire. Some fifty war vessels of the United States were divided into four squadrons, but the secretary of the navy, Benjamin Stoddert, insisted on a strategy where each vessel sailed an independent course. With some sixty to eighty French ships often chasing an equal number of American merchant ships and naval vessels, communications were sometimes extremely difficult. As a result prize vessels on both sides were often retaken. Though some ships never met the enemy, the relatively fast revenue cutters captured more than their share.

One of these valiant little cutters was a brig named *Eagle*. Designed by Josiah Fox and built in Philadelphia in 1798 by William and Abra Brown, the 187-ton vessel was 58 feet along her keel, 20 feet across her beam, with a 9-foot hold and a crew of seventy, including fourteen marines. She mounted fourteen 6-pounders through her gun ports.

The captain of this second *Eagle* was Hugh George Campbell of South Carolina, a demanding but efficient master of his ship. He was not afraid to challenge the secretary of the navy, who deemed *Eagle* ready for sea before he did. Secretary Stoddert ordered the ship to join the twenty-gun *Montezuma*, commanded by Capt. Alexander Murray, and two other vessels in Norfolk. They were to cruise the West Indies to protect American merchantmen. *Montezuma*, however, sailed without *Eagle*. Piqued at Campbell's delay, Secretary Stoddert ordered him to cruise the coasts of Georgia and South Carolina. Campbell's later record in the West Indies raised the secretary's low opinion of him to such heights that in July 1799 Campbell was commissioned a navy master commandant. In October 1800 he was made a Navy captain, which was at that time two grades higher than a captain of the Revenue Service.

In November 1800 Captain Campbell was selected to command the 28-gun frigate *General Greene* in place of Capt. Christopher R. Perry, the father of the commodore, who had been relieved of his command for three months by courtmartial. Captain Campbell was relieved in *Eagle* by Lt. M. Simmones Bunbury of Maryland. During the Barbary wars, Campbell was raised to the command of the frigates *Constellation* and *Constitution* and from 1805 to 1807 was commodore of the Mediterranean Squadron.

In the West Indies from 1798 to 1800, *Eagle* was one of the most successful ships, first in the squadron of Stephen Decatur Sr., later in that of Commo. John Barry. In all, *Eagle* captured five French armed vessels. On two other occasions she assisted the ships *Delaware* and *Baltimore* in taking prizes. In addition, several American merchant vessels captured by the French were retaken by *Eagle*. One of her best captures was the schooner *Bon Pere*, which was renamed *Bee* and used by the American forces.

After Lieutenant Bunbury took command of *Eagle* at the end of December 1800, no further actions involving the cutter were recorded. The undeclared war with France was drawing to a close, and the new captain was told by Secretary Stoddert to "treat public and private armed vessels of France exactly as you find they treat American trading vessels." In a typical postwar economizing action—the war had cost the young government more than $6 million—the second *Eagle* was sold in Baltimore in June 1801 for $10,600.

During the first two decades of United States independence, a diplomatic campaign was waged with England. Its purpose was to wrest from her a fair share of trade with continental

Europe. Grievances increased in the early 1800s. American seamen, while ashore in British ports, were impressed into service on British ships. Since England was at war with France, she maintained her right to search neutral American ships and to seize what she considered to be contraband. It was intolerable, however, for Americans to be treated as colonists thirty years after the Revolution; President James Madison declared war on England on 18 June 1812.

During the first two years of the war, England was too busy with France to spare many ships for the American conflict. When Napoleon was exiled to Elba in the spring of 1814, however, the American coast was blockaded by the full power of the British navy. Revenue cutters, again cooperating with the United States Navy, did their share to protect the eastern seaboard and permit some coastal commerce. By the fall of 1814, several British ships had been captured, but two cutters had been lost to the enemy.

The third cutter to carry the name *Eagle* met the enemy bravely, but she too became a victim of the superior British forces. She was a relatively new schooner-rigged cutter, built in 1809 for the port of New Haven, Connecticut. She was armed with four 4-pounders and a pair of 2-pounders. She was commanded by Capt. Frederick Lee, a noted Connecticut mariner who served as a state representative and founded Lee's Academy in Madison, Connecticut. In 1797, while a merchant captain, he brought the Polish revolutionary war hero Thaddeus Kosciusko back to the United States.

Eagle's job during the War of 1812 was to convoy American ships through Long Island Sound, because British men-of-war often entered the sound in pursuit of American merchant vessels. The sloop *Susan* of New Haven, under Captain Miles, was one of several packets that plied the sound between New Haven and New York. She was returning to her home port in October 1814 with sixteen passengers and a valuable cargo of flour, gunpowder, and dry goods when she was captured by a tender from the British frigate *Pomone*.

Upon hearing of the incident, *Eagle*'s Captain Lee quickly recruited about thirty volunteers in New Haven to reinforce her crew and gave chase. An English 18-gun brig, *Dispatch*, accompanied by her armed tender and a sloop, chased *Eagle*. Light breezes prevented the cutter from outmaneuvering this far superior assembly of guns, so Captain Lee wisely headed for the Long Island shore and beached the cutter beneath a bluff at Negros Head. The crew dragged two of the 4-pounder guns and both of the 2-pounders up onto the bluff to defend their ship.

For six hours a battle raged. When the British were unable to drive the men off the bluff, they tried to destroy the cutter. The adamant men on the hill withstood repeated attacks, which continued through the night. When the wadding for their guns had been used, the crew tore apart the ship's log. They even picked up the enemy's shot from the ground and fired it back. Through it all, the American flag was kept flying, though on two occasions heroic acts were required to keep it so.

What was left of the cutter the next day was refloated by the New Haven volunteers, but *Eagle*'s worn crew could not keep her from the superior forces against them. The third *Eagle* was finally taken by the British.

After the war the Treasury Department commissioned William Doughty, a naval architect and constructor, to design three new classes of cutters to replace those lost during the war. Each design was modeled after the Baltimore clipper. The dimensions of the largest class were to be 79 tons, 69 feet on deck, 19-foot beam, and a 7-foot depth of hold. The fourth and fifth cutters named *Eagle* were constructed from this design.

Little is known about these two cutters. Records show that the first was built in New York in 1816 and was intended for duty in Boston, although she was actually assigned to New Haven throughout her career. The second was probably built in Portsmouth, New Hampshire, in 1824 and stationed in New Haven until 1829. Both cutters were commanded by the same Frederick Lee who was skipper of the third *Eagle* during the War of 1812. While commanding the fourth *Eagle* in 1819, Captain Lee distinguished himself in a daring rescue off Montauk Point, a feat for which he received a handsome silver pitcher engraved with the details of the event. The careers of these two cutters most likely consisted of the routine duties of revenue cutters: ensuring collection of customs duties, capturing contraband, and rescuing life and property endangered by storm or mishaps at sea.

Nearly a century passed before the Coast Guard revived the name *Eagle*, this time for a 100-foot patrol boat. One of thirteen in her class, she was built at Bay City, Michigan, by Defoe Boat and Motor Works and was commissioned 11 November 1925. This *Eagle* arrived at her assignment, New London, Connecticut, a month later. During the ensuing seven years there, she was engaged in enforcing an unpopular law: prohibition.

New London was the home of Base Four, one of the busiest operations in the Coast Guard's rum-chasing activities. An estimated one-third of all liquor smuggled into the country in the 1920s came from Rum Row, that notorious anchorage of supply ships just beyond the three-mile limit. The contact boats swarmed to these ships. The ever-increasing fleet of Coast

Guard craft was kept busy, picketing contact boats and an occasional brazen supply ship until contraband could be seized.

The sixth American *Eagle* had a 210-ton displacement, a 23-foot beam, and an 8-foot draft. She was equipped with two diesel engines, which drove her at 10 knots, not fast enough to catch many of the "rummies." Her armament was a single 3-inch, 23-caliber gun, which was sufficient to stop anything in her range.

A typical incident in *Eagle*'s rum-chasing career occurred in the late 1920s on a dark night, about forty miles south of Nantucket. The *Firelight*, a rum ship, or "black," as such ships were called, was already known to the Coast Guard. A year earlier her operators had been taken, convicted, and released by a typically lenient court. *Eagle* had taken over the trailing of the black from a destroyer, also stationed at Base Four.

The cutter started picketing *Firelight* at midnight. About twenty minutes later *Firelight* swerved, opened her engines, and came at *Eagle*, which was drifting nearby. The cutter quickly backed down to avoid the black, but her starboard side was struck lightly. No serious damage was done to the cutter, but the crew of *Firelight* had misjudged *Eagle*'s strength. *Firelight* began to sink, her underwater planking broken. The eight men on board jumped into the water, where they were picked up by the destroyer and taken to New London to face charges.

In September 1932 the sixth *Eagle* was given a permanent change of station to Charleston, South Carolina. The duties assigned her were similar to those she had been performing in New London. The new presidential administration, however, soon ended the "noble experiment" of prohibition, and the following July other duties were found for the cutter at Charlotte,

New York, and on the shores of Lake Ontario. A year later the ten-year-old ship was sold.

The traditions of service developed by her predecessors are maintained in the seventh cutter bearing the name *Eagle*. Like her forebears and all Coast Guard cutters, the barque *Eagle* performs many missions. She has on numerous occasions been diverted to search and rescue, and medical evacuations. In port she supports the public relations program of the Coast Guard Academy, the Coast Guard, and the nation. During the nation's bicentennial, *Eagle* served as host ship for Operation Sail. Her primary mission, however, is to train cadets and officer candidates in seamanship, navigation, damage control, engineering, and shipboard watch standing. This mission emphasizes the Coast Guard's firm belief in the value of sail training even in an age of gas turbines.

The training of cadets began in May 1877, aboard the topsail schooner *J. C. Dobbin*. Capt. J. A. Henriques had two lieutenants and a few petty officers to assist him in instruction. The curriculum was composed of seamanship and navigation, and the ship sailed for five months each year between the United States and Bermuda. When she moored in New Bedford, Massachusetts, for the winter, academic subjects were added to the curriculum, and the first civilian professor was added to the staff.

The following year, *J. C. Dobbin* was replaced by the 106-foot barque *Chase*. New Bedford remained the home port of *Chase* from 1878 to 1890. After the suspension of "academy training," which lasted from 1890 to 1894, *Chase* moored for the winter in various southern ports until 1900, when winter quarters were established ashore at Arundel Cove, near Baltimore, Maryland.

Coming ashore did not mean giving up sail training. *Chase* served until 1907 as the Academy's training ship. European cruises, which had started in the 1880s, were continued. When *Chase* was converted into a barracks ship in Arundel Cove in 1907, she was replaced by a former Naval Academy practice ship, *Bancroft*, which the Coast Guard renamed *Itasca*.

The next cadet training ship was *Alexander Hamilton*, the third ship to be named after the founder of the Coast Guard. She had formerly been the naval gunboat *Vicksburg*, which saw service in China after her launching in 1898 and was later used as one of the state of Washington's naval militia practice vessels. She was turned over to the Coast Guard in 1921 and remained in service until 1930. Meanwhile, the Academy had moved from Arundel Cove to New London, Connecticut, situating first at historic Fort Trumbull in 1910 and moving to its present site in 1932. Until 1954 the mainmast from the cutter *Hamilton* served as the Academy's flagpole.

The Academy did not own a large training ship from 1930 until 1946, when it acquired the German training barque *Horst Wessel*, today's *Eagle*. During that period sail training was carried out on a fleet of smaller craft: a two-masted Gloucester fishing schooner, *J. C. Dobbin II*, renamed *Chase*; a 65-foot schooner yacht, *Curlew*; the famous three-masted, 185-foot ocean racing schooner *Atlantic*; and a number of small yachts and dinghies. In these, cadets learned the rudiments of seamanship.

A most fortunate aid to Academy sail training occurred when the Danish full-rigged training ship *Danmark* was placed by her captain, Knud L. Hansen, at the disposal of the United States. This came as a result of Hitler's invasion of Denmark. From January 1942 to September 1945, officers and crew taught cadets to handle the 700-ton ship in every sea condition. *Danmark*'s mainmast still bears a bronze plaque commemorating her wartime service in the U.S. Coast Guard.

When World War II ended, the Danes said fond good-byes, and the Academy looked for another training ship. Such a ship was found in Germany. After the war, there were three German barques to be shared by the Allied victors as war reparations: *Gorch Fock* went to the Soviet Union and was renamed *Tovarisch*; *Albert Leo Schlageter* went to Brazil but was later sold to Portugal and became *Sagres II*; and *Horst Wessel* went to the United States and became the seventh *Eagle*.

Mircea, a Romanian vessel, is a fourth sister ship, also built in Germany. The fifth sister is *Gorch Fock II*, built by the Germans in 1958 using the plan of *Horst Wessel*. Some of the rigging used to build *Gorch Fock II* came from another training barque, *Herbert Norkus*, which was never completed because of World War II. The last time all five sisters were together was in 1976 in New York City.

The seventh *Eagle*, a 1,816-ton, 295-foot barque, was built in Hamburg in 1936 by Blohm and Voss. Named *Horst Wessel* after an early lieutenant of Hitler's, she served the German navy for ten years as a training ship, making cruises to the Canary Islands and West Indies. During World War II she operated in the Baltic Sea, sometimes transporting supplies to and refugees from East Prussia. Her log records that she fired at Allied planes at least once, and that Hitler's birthday was dutifully observed on board.

In January 1946 Cdr. Gordon McGowan, who had been teaching seamanship to cadets, was ordered to head a group of ten officers and Coast Guardsmen as the nucleus of a crew to sail *Eagle* to the Academy from Bremerhaven, Germany. Refitting the ship for sea in war-torn Germany took five months, and German sailors were then recruited to supplement the Coast Guard crew. The return trip was made in June and July, by the triangular Madeira–Bermuda–New York route, along which the inexperienced crew sailed into a hurricane. But the seventh *Eagle* dispelled any doubts the skipper might have had about her seaworthiness. Although he brought his ship into New York Harbor with unseamanlike shreds of sail draped over her spars, the ship and crew arrived safely.

When the Coast Guard took over this *Eagle* in Bremerhaven, the figurehead was a handsome carved eagle. Its talons held a wreath with a swastika inside, the symbol of the Nazis. The eagle remained, but the swastika was replaced by the shield of the United States Coast Guard. Over the years the figurehead has been replaced several times. The original figurehead is currently displayed at the Coast Guard Museum at the U.S Coast Guard Academy. The current figurehead was fabricated in 1977 of mahogany with a stainless steel rod, ensuring a longevity equal to that of *Eagle*.

Each year since 1948 *Eagle* has been the backbone of the Academy's summer professional training program. Alone or accompanied by regular cutters, she has sailed the entire North Atlantic and visited almost every major port in Europe, on the East Coast, and in the Caribbean. On occasion she has sailed through the Panama Canal to the West Coast. In 1987–88 she made her longest voyage, a 30,000-mile round-trip visit to the South Pacific and Australia to celebrate the Australian bicentennial. Whenever her schedule has permitted, she has participated in sail training association races, competing against other "tall ships" from Europe, South America, and even Asia.

On the Fourth of July in 1976, *Eagle*, as host vessel, led the parade of tall ships into New York Harbor for Operation Sail '76 to celebrate the United States bicentennial. In 1986 "America's Tall Ship" was again proudly the host vessel for

Operation Sail '86, sailing into New York Harbor for the centennial of the Statue of Liberty. This celebration coincided with *Eagle*'s fiftieth anniversary. For her sixtieth anniversary in 1996, *Eagle* visited her birthplace, Hamburg, Germany, and continued on to St. Petersburg, Russia, to commemorate the four hundredth anniversary of the Russian Navy. The arrival of the new millennium saw Eagle host more than twenty-five international and domestic tall ships in numerous United States ports for Operation Sail 2000.

Some 141 cadets or officer candidates can be trained at a time in *Eagle*, about ten times as many as in a more modern cutter. This is an economic advantage, of course, but the main reason for sail training is the intimate knowledge of sea and wind that a cadet acquires from *Eagle*. In addition, upperclass cadets on board gain experience in leadership essential to their performance as officers.

This philosophy of sail training is reflected in the U.S. Coast Guard Academy mission:

> *To graduate young men and women with sound bodies, stout hearts, and alert minds, with a liking for the sea and its lore, and with that high sense of honor, loyalty, and obedience which goes with trained initiative and leadership; well-grounded in seamanship, the sciences, and the amenities; and strong in the resolve to be worthy of the traditions of commissioned officers in the United States Coast Guard in the service of their country and humanity.*

That is the mission too of *Eagle*, a name engraved deeply in the traditions of the Coast Guard, traditions nearly as old as the United States.

CHAPTER 2

Eagle's Construction

To fully appreciate the beauty of *Eagle* and to understand the traditions of mastering the sea under sail, one must first learn the vessel, her rig, and the language of the sea. Many of the terms and commands described in the following paragraphs have deep roots in the lore of square-rigger sailors and cuttermen of the past. By using proper nautical terminology, commands can be given safely and will be correctly understood. Thus, it is important for personnel to quickly learn to describe the various parts of *Eagle* and the commands used in all evolutions. In the following chapters, important nautical terms have been italicized or boldfaced. The glossary contains definitions of many commonly used nautical terms not defined in this text.

Hull Construction

Eagle is constructed of German steel, using the transverse framing system. The details of construction are very similar to U.S. shipbuilding practices of the 1930s. When *Eagle* was built, the technique of full welding had not yet been developed. In general the steel plate seams are riveted and the butts are welded. Fittings are generally bolted while strength members, such as knees and gussets, are welded to the frames. The plating is approximately ½ inch thick.

There are two full-length steel decks, a platform deck below those, and a raised forecastle (pronounced, and often spelled, as "foc's'le") and quarterdeck. The weather decks have a 3-inch teak deck laid on top of steel. The second deck is constructed of ¼-inch steel covered with poured resin decking. The platform deck and the tank tops are painted steel.

The second deck is the damage control deck. There are nine watertight bulkheads that run from the bilges to the main deck. These bulkheads have watertight doors on the second and third decks and are located at frames 10, 25, 37, 49, 63, 75, 90, 107, and 112.

Compartment Nomenclature

Figures 1a–1f show the various compartments in *Eagle*. The compartments are designated, in accordance with standard U.S. Coast Guard and Navy practice, using three sets of numbers and a letter. The first number indicates the deck on which the compartment is located. The main deck is 1, the second deck 2, and so forth. Decks above the main deck begin with 0 (zero); thus, on board *Eagle* the bridge is the 01 deck, the top of the pilothouse is the 02 deck, and so on. The second number of the compartment number indicates the frame nearest the forward end of the compartment. The final number indicates whether the compartment is to port or starboard. Compartments to starboard are designated by odd numbers; those to port have even numbers. Compartments that are amidships or extend across the entire width of the *ship* are designated by 0. Outboard

Figure 1a. Watertight Subdivision and Damage Control Fittings

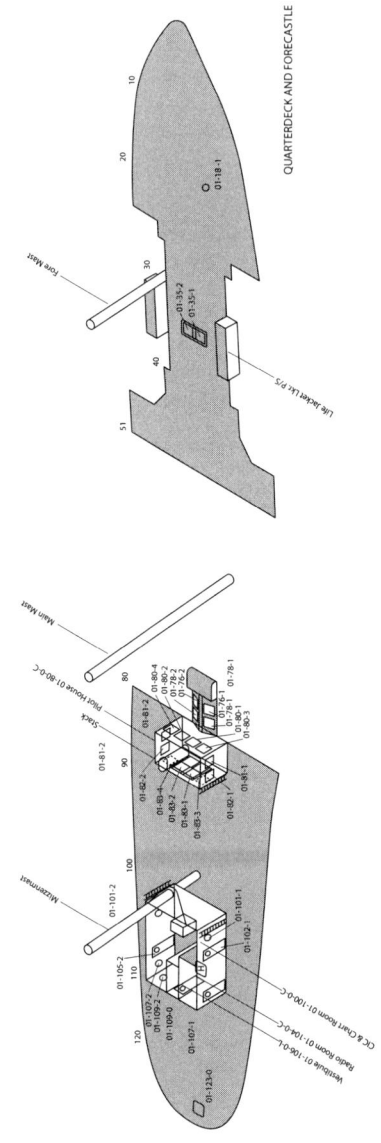

Figure 1b. Watertight Subdivision and Damage Control Fittings (continued)

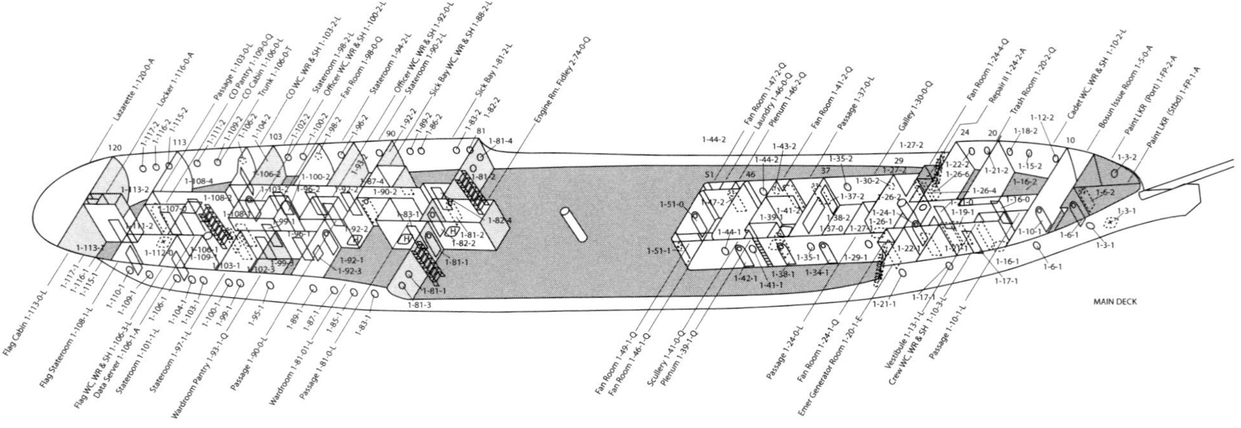

Figure 1c. Watertight Subdivision and Damage Control Fittings (continued)

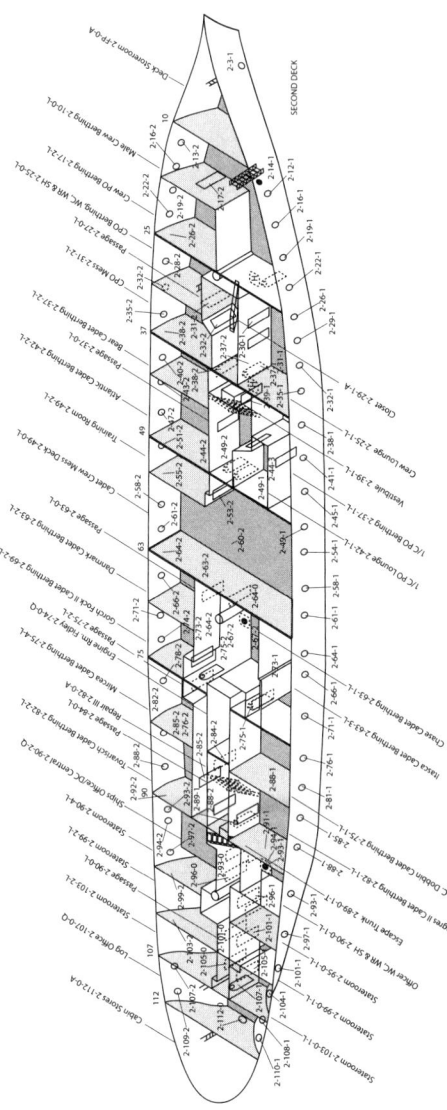

Figure 1d. Watertight Subdivision and Damage Control Fittings (continued)

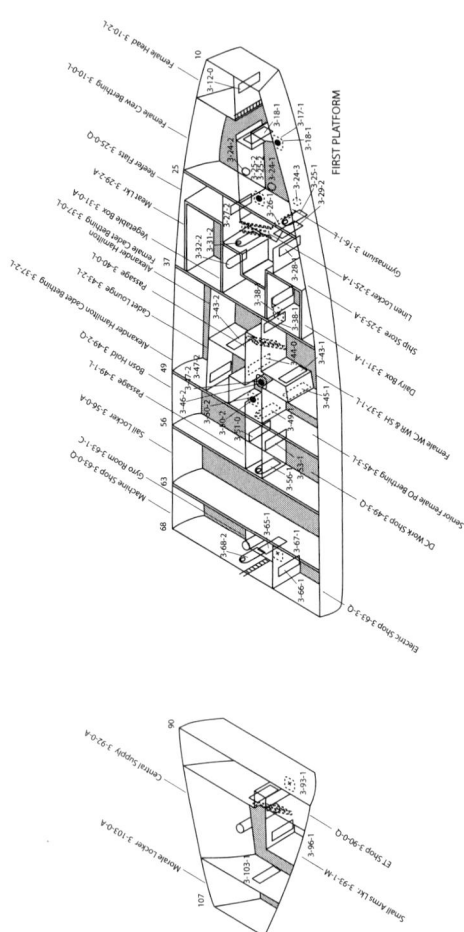

Figure 1e. Watertight Subdivision and Damage Control Fittings (continued)

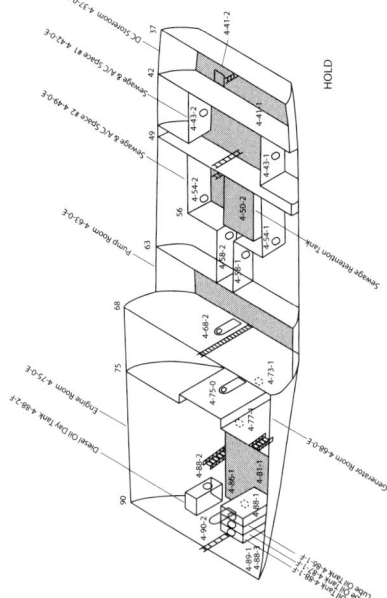

Figure 1f. Watertight Subdivision and Damage Control Fittings (continued)

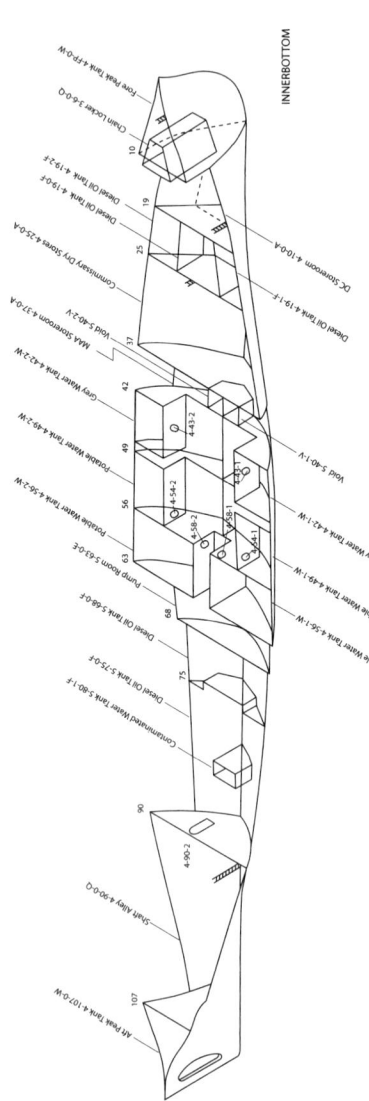

INNERBOTTOM

Fore Peak Tank 4-FP-0-W
Chain Locker 3-6-0-Q
Diesel Oil Tank 4-19-2-F
Diesel Oil Tank 4-19-0-F
DC Storeroom 4-10-0-A
Commissary (Dry Stores) 4-25-0-A
Diesel Oil Tank 4-19-1-F
MAA Storeroom 4-37-0-A
Void 5-40-2-V
Grey Water Tank 4-42-2-W
Void 5-40-1-V
Potable Water Tank 4-49-2-W
W Water Tank 4-42-1-W
Potable Water Tank 4-56-2-W
He Water Tank 4-49-1-W
Pump Room 5-63-0-E
He Water Tank 4-56-1-W
Diesel Oil Tank 5-68-0-F
Diesel Oil Tank 5-75-0-F
Contaminated Water Tank 5-80-1-F
Shaft Alley 4-90-0-Q
Aft Peak Tank 4-107-0-W

4-43-2
4-54-2
4-58-2
4-58-1
4-64-1
4-90-2

10
19
25
33
42
49
56
63
69
75
96
107

compartments have final numbers greater than compartments closer to the centerline.

The letter that follows the three numbers indicates the use of the compartment. For example, *L* is used for living spaces, *E* for engineering spaces, and *F* for fuel tanks. The compartment number of the engine room is 4-75-0-E. This indicates that it is on the fourth deck, its forward bulkhead is at frame 75, it extends across the entire width of the vessel, and it is used as an engineering space.

Compartment numbers, their locations, and their uses must be quickly learned. In an emergency anyone may be called upon to assist damage control parties in any part of the vessel. It is also very important that all hands learn escape routes from every compartment in the vessel. These escape routes should be memorized and must become second nature, even in the dark. A competent mariner is able to determine which space is above, below, forward, aft, port, and starboard of his or her location at any time.

Watertight Integrity

Buoyancy and stability are two essential attributes of any ship; they must be preserved if she is to continue to float and to sail. Numerous compartments with watertight boundaries and proper distribution of weight ensure that the vessel has both buoyancy and stability.

Flooding of water into a compartment that is designed to be dry will decrease buoyancy. It is also likely to have an adverse effect upon stability by introducing weight in the wrong place. Therefore, a prime concern in ship construction is watertight integrity. Ideally all watertight bulkheads are continuous with no possible sources of leakage: no doors, hatches, port lights, vent ducts, or cable runs through bulkheads.

There must be access to each space, however, and habitability demands cable runs and ventilation. So designers have to compromise between watertight integrity and operational usability. They break the watertight boundaries to provide the necessary access.

Still, the ship must be capable of being made watertight in the event of a collision or grounding. Water that might accidentally enter the hull must be prevented from flooding progressively from one compartment to the next. In order to maintain watertight integrity in boundaries containing openings, each fitting is provided with a watertight designation. If all fittings were closed, the ship should be watertight. There would be no access, however. Each opening of a watertight fitting reduces the total watertight integrity somewhat. To have knowledge of the extent to which it has been diminished, there must be a record of what fittings are open. The watertight integrity maintained in U.S. Coast Guard and Navy vessels at a particular time is called its material condition.

Although this procedure maintains good control over watertight integrity, it can be more restrictive than is needed outside of wartime or very heavy weather. Under some circumstances it is reasonable to allow frequently used access doors to be opened. Personnel are close enough to the fittings to close them promptly in case of accident.

There are three different standard material conditions that may be prescribed for *Eagle,* depending upon the degree of watertight integrity required.

1. *Material condition XRAY.* The most relaxed condition; suitable for daytime while in port.

2. *Material condition YOKE.* An intermediate condition used at night when in port and at all times under way.

3. *Material condition ZEBRA.* The most secure material condition in which the ship can continue to operate; suitable for extremely heavy weather, attack, or when damage is imminent.

To determine what fittings are to be open or closed in each of the material conditions, each fitting is classified according to its function and importance. A letter (*X, Y, Z,* or *W**) indicating the classification is attached to each fitting and the following closure table is applied.

	Classification			
Material Condition	X	Y	Z	W
XRAY	Closed	Open	Open	Open
YOKE	Closed	Closed	Open	Open
ZEBRA	Closed	Closed	Closed	Open

* Material condition WILLIAM fittings control a ship's ventilation on board naval vessels; they are only secured as a precaution against chemical, biological, or radiological threats.

A label with a circle around it is designated as *Circle XRAY (YOKE, ZEBRA).* This circle indicates that the fitting (usually hatches and watertight doors) may be opened for passage without obtaining permission from the officer of the deck (OOD) as long as the fitting is immediately secured again.

Whenever it becomes necessary to open a fitting that is supposed to be closed according to the material condition in effect, permission must be obtained from the OOD. When requesting permission, you must give the name and rank/rate of the person making the request, the type of fitting, the number of the fitting, the classification of the fitting, and the reason for the request. When permission is given to open a fitting, this information is logged with the time in the Damage Control Closure Log. The closure of a fitting is reported promptly and is also logged.

Principal Measurements of *Eagle*

Length overall	295 ft.
Length without bowsprit	277 ft.
Length at waterline	233 ft.
Beam	39.1 ft.
Freeboard	9.1 ft.
Draft (fully loaded)	17.0 ft.
Displacement (fully loaded)	1,816 tn.
Ballast (lead pigs)	344 tn.
Fuel oil	24,215 gal.
Water	56,140 gal.
Height of fore truck (above waterline)	147.3 ft.
Height of main truck	147.3 ft.
Height of mizzen truck	132 ft.
Sail area	21,350 sq. ft.
Auxiliary power (Caterpillar diesel)	1,000 hp
Speed under power	11 kts.
Speed under sail	Up to 17.5 kts.
Anchors (Navy stockless)	3,500 lb. (port); 3,850 lb. (starboard)
Number of sails	23

CHAPTER 3

Masts, Spars, and Standing Rigging

Masts and Spars

The lower masts, topmasts, topgallant (pronounced "t'gallant") masts, royal masts, bowsprit, yards, booms, and mizzen gaffs of *Eagle* are all made of hollow steel tubes; they are also known as spars. The foremast is *stepped on* the second deck, the mainmast is stepped on the keel, and the mizzenmast is stepped on the platform deck above *shaft alley*.

The foremast and the mainmast and their *yards* are identical. As shown in figure 2, *Eagle* follows the rigging practices of large sailing vessels in their final stage of development. The foremast and its topmast are actually one spar, as are the mainmast and its topmast. They are rigged as the older vessels were, however: the shrouds come in under the tops, where a new system of topmast shrouds originates.

The two sections of the mast retain their original names. For example, on the mainmast the nomenclature is "mainmast" from the deck to the top, and "main-topmast" from the top to the crosstrees. The same applies to the foremast. The topgallant and royal masts are also combined into one hollow steel spar. The topgallant shrouds terminate about halfway up the spar. The portion above the topgallant shrouds is known as the royal mast. The following table gives the names and weights of the individual spars.

Figure 2. Fore and Main Mast Structure and Standing Rigging

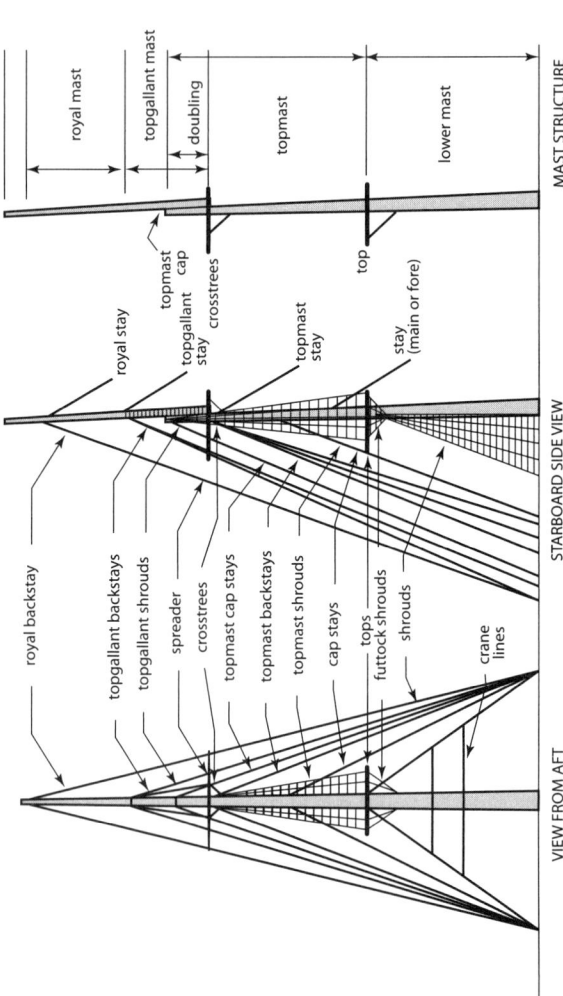

Measurements of *Eagle*'s Spars

Name of Spar	Length	Weight
Bowsprit	43 ft.	7,300 lb.
Topgallant masts	49 ft.	2,128 lb.
Fore and main yards	79 ft.	6,380 lb.
Lower topsail yards	72 ft.	4,840 lb.
Upper topsail yards	63 ft.	3,520 lb.
Topgallant yards	50 ft.	1,700 lb.
Royal yards	38 ft.	884 lb.
Mizzen upper gaff	35 ft.	994 lb.
Mizzen lower gaff	43.5 ft.	1150 lb.
Mizzen boom	54 ft.	2,200 lb.

Standing Rigging

In any sailing vessel there are two types of rigging. *Standing rigging* supports the masts and generally does not move. On board *Eagle*, standing rigging is colored black, white, or bare stainless steel. *Running rigging* is used to *set*, *douse*, and *trim* the sails. On board *Eagle*, running rigging is generally brown-colored three-strand polypropylene *line*. Running rigging is described in chapter 4.

Since a majority of standing rigging must support the masts against the tremendous force of the wind on the sails, it is made of high-strength wire *rope*. Standing rigging is not adjustable, except through *turnbuckles* (also known as *bottles*), and much of it is *wormed, parceled, and served* to protect it from rust and corrosion.

The three most important types of standing rigging are *stays*, *shrouds*, and *backstays*.

1. *Stays* provide fore-and-aft support for the masts, leading forward from the mast to the deck, bowsprit, or next forward mast. They counteract the *rake* of the mast and provide almost all of the support for the masts when the sails are *aback*. Since there are only a few stays for each mast, it can be dangerous to be *caught aback* in high winds.

The *bobstay* is a steel rod that runs from the bow, just above the waterline, to the *bowsprit*. The bobstay gives support to the bowsprit and allows it to take the strain of the stays that support the foremast. The *martingale stay* runs from the *dolphin striker* to the stem, providing additional support for the bowsprit.

As illustrated in figure 3, the stays are named for the part of the mast they lead to. The headsails and staysails are *bent* to these stays. In general the staysails are named for the stay that they are bent to.

2. *Shrouds* provide athwartship support for the masts. *Eagle* has three sets of shrouds on the foremast and the mainmast, two sets on the mizzenmast, and one set on the bowsprit. The lower shrouds (see fig. 3) lead from the deck to the *tops* (the lower platforms, named for the "Fighting Tops," where marines were stationed in battle during the Age of Sail).

The topmast shrouds lead from the tops to just below the *crosstrees* (the upper platform). The topgallant shrouds (mainmast and foremast) lead from the crosstrees to just below the *truck* (top of the mast).

Futtock shrouds are steel rods leading from the futtock band below the tops to the edge of the tops. They provide a

Figure 3. Standing Rigging

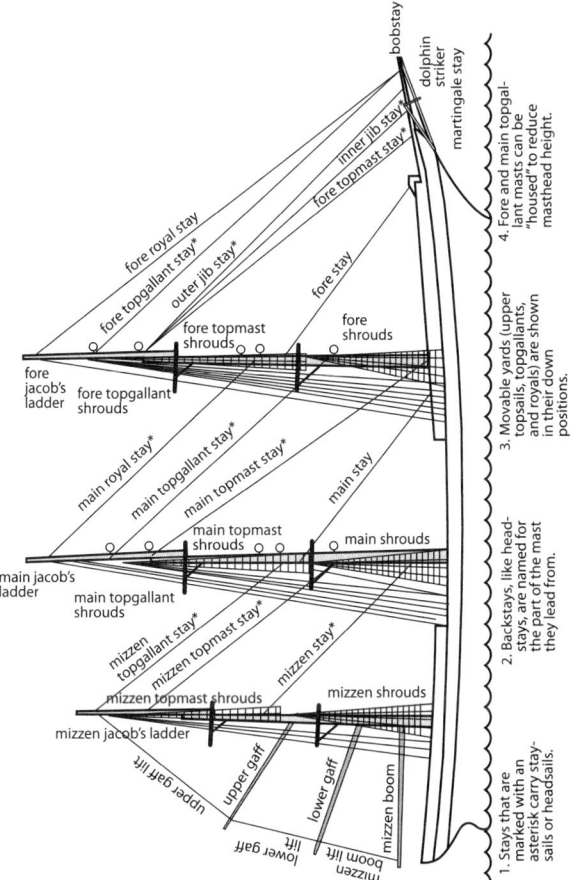

1. Stays that are marked with an asterisk carry staysails or headsails.

2. Backstays, like headstays, are named for the part of the mast they lead from.

3. Movable yards (upper topsails, topgallants, and royals) are shown in their down positions.

4. Fore and main topgallant masts can be "housed" to reduce masthead height.

bobstay
dolphin striker
martingale stay

inner jib stay*
fore topmast stay*

fore royal stay
fore topgallant stay*
outer jib stay*

fore stay

fore topmast shrouds
fore shrouds

fore jacob's ladder
fore topgallant shrouds

main royal stay*
main topgallant stay*
main topmast stay*
main stay

main topmast shrouds
main shrouds

main jacob's ladder
main topgallant shrouds

mizzen topgallant stay*
mizzen topmast stay*
mizzen stay*

mizzen topmast shrouds
mizzen shrouds

mizzen jacob's ladder

upper gaff lift
upper gaff
lower gaff lift
lower gaff
mizzen boom lift
mizzen boom

foundation for the topmast shrouds and connect the topmast shrouds with the lower masts.

Ratlines are *seized* to the shrouds to form a means by which personnel may lay aloft.

Crane lines are wire ropes that lead from the shrouds athwartships to the masts. They provide a footing for personnel handling the staysails.

3. *Backstays* provide diagonal support to the after side of the masts and provide the bulk of the support for the masts when sails are set.

Other types of standing rigging include *footropes*, which are wire ropes hung from *stirrups* under the yards to provide footing while working out on the yards; *flemish horses*, which are loops of wire rope providing footing at the *yardarms*; and fixed *lifts*, which support the upper three yards when the sails are not set.

CHAPTER 4

Running Rigging and Sails

In a good breeze *Eagle*'s twenty-three sails drive her faster than her auxiliary engine. The sails are set, doused, and trimmed using running rigging. The task of memorizing the location and use of more than 190 lines may at first seem overwhelming, but it is readily surmountable with some effort and common sense. The lines can be grouped into a handful of uses; their locations are logically determined by their functions. In addition, most lines are paired and located similarly on the foremast and mainmast. To understand these functions it is first necessary to examine *Eagle*'s sail plan (see fig. 4).

Square Sails

Eagle has ten square sails. The respective sails on the foremast and mainmast are almost identical. The "top" of a square sail is the *head*. The head of a square sail is attached to the *jackstay* on its yard with *robands*. *Earings* secure the upper corners of the sail using hooks on the jackstay to keep the head of the sail taut. The sides of a square sail are the *leeches*, the bottom is the *foot*, and the lower corners of the sail are the *clews* (see fig. 5). Running along the outer edges of the sail is the *boltrope* and a wide *tabling* of sailcloth, which helps shape the sail and give it strength.

1. *Sheets* are lines attached to the clews and are used to haul the foot down to the yard below when setting sail. The section of sheet that is led through the *cheek block* at the yardarm is made of chain to resist *chafing*. The remainder the sheet is wire rope with a single-sheave block attached at the bitter end. All square sail sheets, except those on the *courses*, are belayed to the *fife rails*. The sheets for the courses are led aft from each sail, since the course does not have a yard below it (see fig. 6).

2. *Clewlines* are also attached to the clews of the sail, but they oppose the sheets. Clewlines lead up to the yard on which the sail is bent rather than down to the yard below. Just as the sheets are used to haul the sail down when setting, the clewlines (*clew-garnet* on the courses) are used to haul the sail up when taking it in. All square sail clewlines, except those on the courses, are belayed to the *pinrails*. (See fig. 6).

3. *Buntlines* are also used to take in sail. If just the clewlines were used, the sail would belly out in the wind so that it could not be furled. In heavy winds it would *luff* violently, potentially causing damage to gear or injury to personnel. The buntlines run from the foot of the sail through *bull's eyes* on the sail, which allow the buntlines to gather the sail up to the yard in several small bights. *Lizards* at the head of the sail provide *fairleads* for the buntlines to run inboard to the mast, thence out to the pinrails for all square sails but the courses (see fig. 7).

4. *Leechlines* are used on the courses because their leeches are so long that they are difficult to handle when taking in sail. These lines lead from the middle of the leeches up to the yard. On the upper four square sails on each mast, the leechlines and outer buntlines are combined into a single *bunt-leechline*.

Figure 4. Sail Plan of USCGC *Eagle*

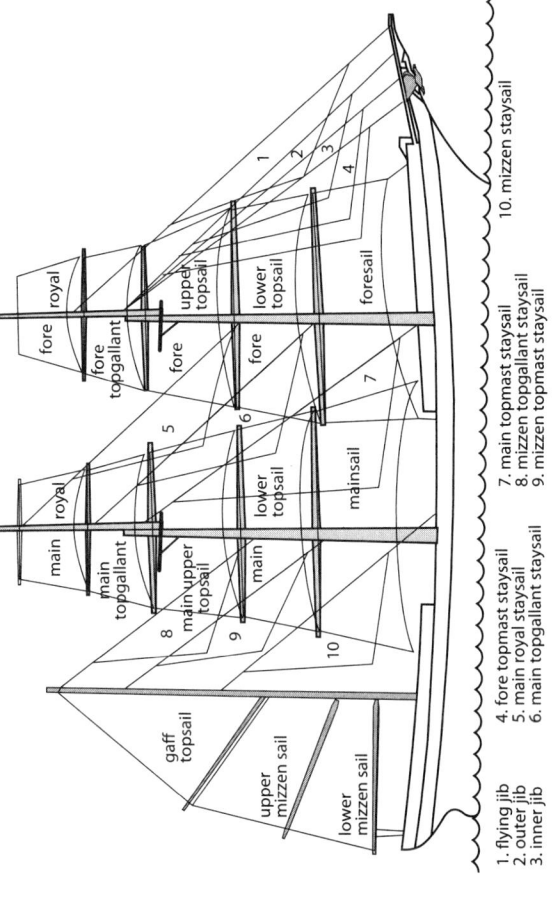

1. flying jib
2. outer jib
3. inner jib
4. fore topmast staysail
5. main royal staysail
6. main topgallant staysail
7. main topmast staysail
8. mizzen topgallant staysail
9. mizzen topmast staysail
10. mizzen staysail

fore royal
fore topgallant
upper topsail
fore
lower topsail
fore
foresail

main royal
main topgallant
main upper topsail
main
lower topsail
mainsail

gaff topsail
upper mizzen sail
lower mizzen sail

Figure 5. Square Sail and Yard Detail

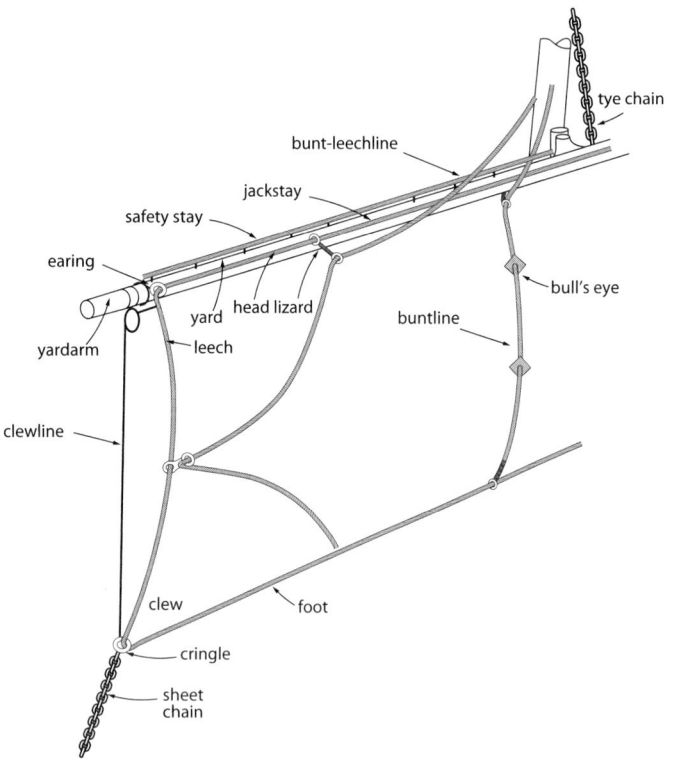

Figure 6. Square Sail Sheets and Chewlines

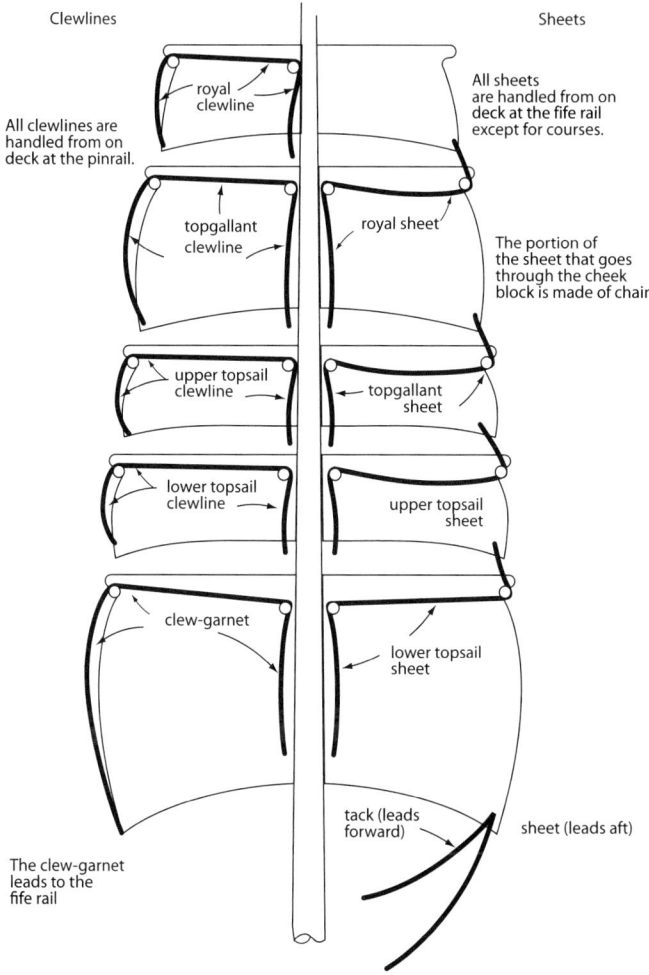

Clewlines

Sheets

royal clewline

All sheets are handled from on deck at the fife rail except for courses.

All clewlines are handled from on deck at the pinrail.

topgallant clewline

royal sheet

The portion of the sheet that goes through the cheek block is made of chain.

upper topsail clewline

topgallant sheet

lower topsail clewline

upper topsail sheet

clew-garnet

lower topsail sheet

tack (leads forward)

sheet (leads aft)

The clew-garnet leads to the fife rail

Figure 7. Square Sail Detail: Set and Doused

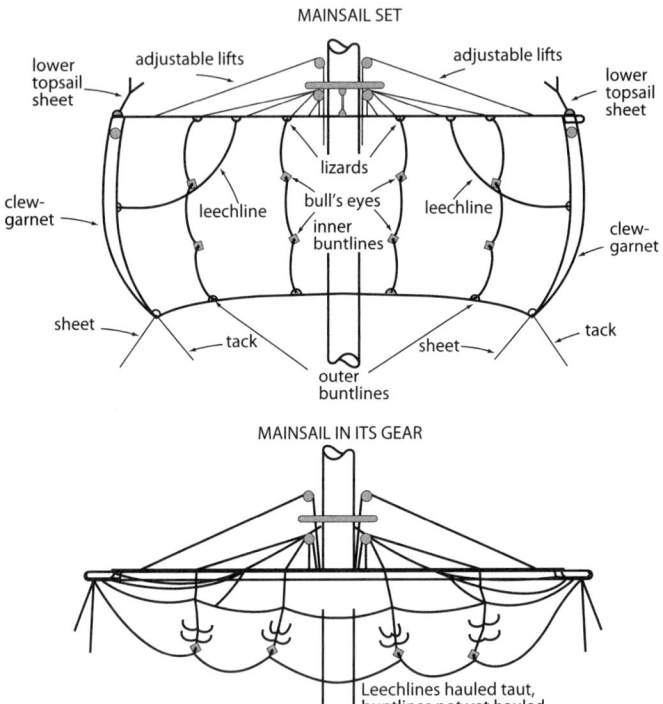

MAINSAIL SET

lower topsail sheet

adjustable lifts

adjustable lifts

lower topsail sheet

lizards

clew-garnet

leechline

bull's eyes

inner buntlines

leechline

clew-garnet

sheet

tack

sheet

tack

outer buntlines

MAINSAIL IN ITS GEAR

Leechlines hauled taut, buntlines not yet hauled taut.

5. *Tacks* are used only on the courses. Unlike the upper square sails, the courses are not set onto a lower yard. Thus, it is impossible to control the clew of the sail with a single line, for when braced sharp, the lead of the weather sheet is excessively long. (The weather sheet is the sheet on the *weather*, or windward, side of the ship.) Tacks are connected to the course clews. In setting the courses, the tacks (which lead forward) and sheets (which lead aft) are used to trim the sail. When braced three points or greater, the weather leech of the sail is flattened using a *tack jigger*, a threefold *purchase* attached to the course clew and to a *padeye* on deck.

6. Square sail *halyards* are used to raise the upper three yards when setting sail. The upper three square sails are set by hauling the foot down to the lower yard *(sheeting home)* and then hauling the yard up until the sail sets properly. The upper yards are movable for several reasons. Having the yard down when the sail is not set lowers the center of gravity of the vessel and thus improves *Eagle's* stability in a seaway. When a yard is *in its lifts* it is secure even in the roughest of sea conditions. It is also much easier to set and douse square sails with a movable yard. When a yard is in its fixed lifts, sheeting home is relatively easy since the sail will still spill most of the wind as the clews are hauled down to the yard below. The sail can then be fully set by hauling on a single line with a large mechanical advantage, the halyard, instead of two sheets whose mechanical advantage is much less.

Additionally, heavy weather or unexpected squalls often require taking in the upper square sails quickly. This can be done easily with a movable yard by easing the halyard and hauling the yard down with the clewlines. When the yard settles into its fixed lifts, most of the wind will be spilled, making *clewing up* much easier. *Furling is* also safer since the yard is more secure in its fixed lifts.

Headsails and Staysails

Eagle has six staysails and four headsails. Metal *hanks* are used to bend a sail to its stay. The leading edge of the sail is the *luff*. The lower edge is the foot, and the trailing edge is the leech. The uppermost point of the sail, to which the halyard is bent, is the head; the lowest point, to which the tack pendant is attached, is the tack; the clew is the remaining point, to which the sheet is attached. The edges of the sail, as with square sails, are reinforced with boltrope and a tabling of sailcloth. The panels of sailcloth parallel either the leech or the foot and are joined at the *miter seam*, which runs from the clew to the center of the luff (see fig. 8).

Three types of lines control the headsails and staysails: halyards, sheets, and *downhauls*. A tack pendant secures the tack to the mast on the staysails and to the bowsprit on the headsails. The tack pendant is used to keep the sail at the proper distance up the stay; it is permanently attached and not adjustable.

1. Staysail and headsail *halyards* are bent to the head of a sail and are used to set a sail by hauling the head up the stay.

2. *Sheets*, as on square sails, are attached to the clew and are used for trimming. The headsails have two sheets each (one for each side), and thus their sheets can be shifted without dousing the sail. In contrast, the staysails have a single sheet pendant that must be shifted from side to side depending on the tack *Eagle* is sailing on. It is impractical to rig dual sheets for the

Figure 8. Staysail and Headsail Detail

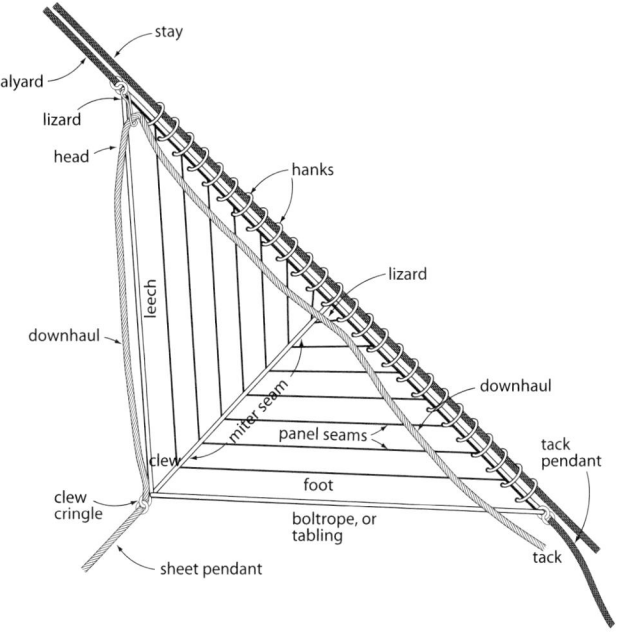

staysails since they are set higher above the deck than the head-sails; therefore, it would be difficult to haul the sheet over the lower stays from the deck.

The staysail sheets are made up of two parts. A rope sheet pendant is permanently shackled to the clew of the sail. A sheet tackle is shackled to an eye on deck and led through a lizard at the end of the pendant. In shifting the sheets the pendant is hauled up and over any lower stays by *topmen* stationed in the tops. The tackle on the opposite side is then led through the sheet pendant lizard.

3. *Downhauls*, as the name implies, are used for hauling stay-sails and headsails down the stays when dousing. They lead from the clew through a lizard at the head of the sail and then down to the fife rails for the staysails (the *dograil* for the head-sails). This arrangement allows for better control of the sail when dousing. Hauling on the downhaul will raise the clew of the sail up to the head, causing it to spill its wind; continuing to haul will pull the sail down the stay.

Lower and Upper Mizzens

The lower and upper mizzensails are rigged in a manner anal-ogous to that of the square sails. Several parts of the mizzen-sails bear the same names as those of the square sails. Unique to the mizzensails, however, the upper aft corner of the sail is known as the *peak* and the upper forward corner as the *throat*. The lower forward corner is the tack and the lower aft corner is the clew (see fig. 9). The running rigging for the mizzen is as follows.

Figure 9. Mizzensail Detail

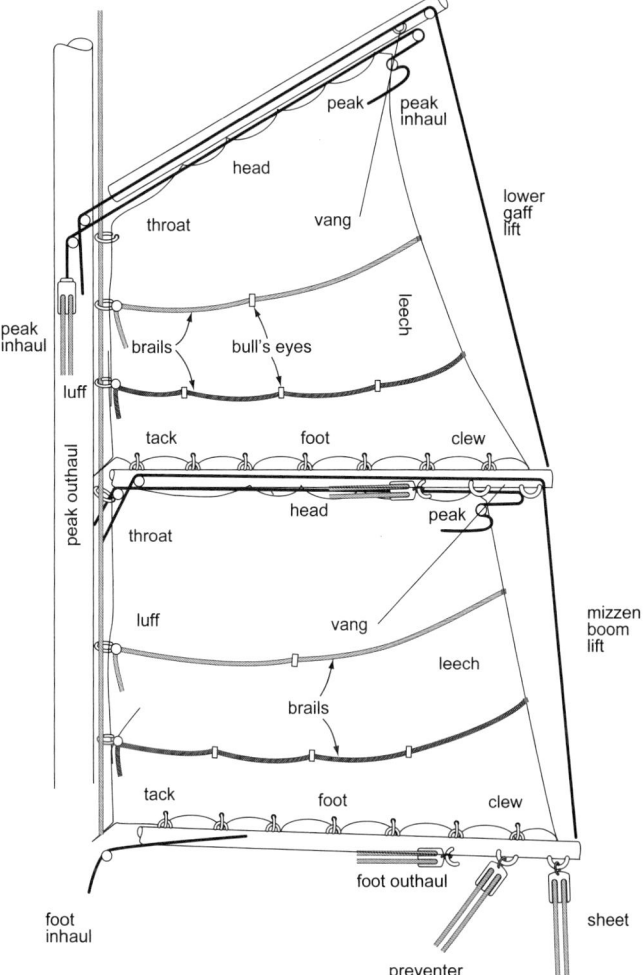

1. *Outhauls* are similar to the sheets of the square sails and are used to haul the mizzensails out to the end of the *boom* and *gaffs* when setting.

2. *Inhauls* are likewise similar to the clewlines of the square sails and oppose the outhauls. They are used to haul the head and foot of the mizzensails into the mast when *brailing in*.

3. The *brails* are similar to the buntlines on the square sails and are used to control the body of the mizzensails when brailing in. Brails are rigged on both sides of the sail.

4. The *mizzen sheet* is a threefold purchase that leads from padeyes on the fantail to the end of the boom. It is used to control the boom.

5. The *preventer* is a purchase used to oppose the sheet. Since the sheet leads from *amidships* on the fantail, it cannot control the swing of the boom. If *Eagle* gets caught aback and the boom starts to swing, the tremendous momentum developed by more than a ton of gear swinging out of control could easily tear the sail or even rip the boom from the mast. In sailing parlance, the preventer prevents uncontrolled *jibes.* Since only a single preventer is rigged, it must be shifted to the opposite side whenever *Eagle* comes about. When the boom is amidships, it can be secured without the preventer by using just the mizzen sheet.

6. *Vangs* are used to control the upper and lower gaffs. They prevent the gaffs from *slatting about* (moving uncontrollably), particularly when the mizzensails are not set. When the mizzensails are set, the movement of the gaffs is controlled by the mizzen sheet, to which they are connected through the leeches of the sails. In such cases the vangs are used mainly for trimming.

Gaff Topsail

The gaff topsail, like the rest of the mizzensails, is unique, although the lines function exactly as in the other twenty-two sails of *Eagle*. The parts of the gaff topsail bear the same names as those of a staysail (see fig. 10).

1. The *halyard* is attached to the head of the sail and is used for setting (as with a staysail).

2. The *sheet* is attached to the clew of the sail and is used to haul the clew to the end of the upper gaff when setting.

3. The *clewline*, like that of a square sail, opposes the sheet and is used to haul the clew of the sail in when dousing. It is also similar to the downhaul of a staysail.

4. The *tacks* are attached to the tack of the sail and are used to adjust the set of the luff and foot of the sail. Two tacks are rigged, one on either side of the upper gaff, so that the tack of the sail can be shifted to either side of the upper gaff without sending personnel aloft.

Lifts

Lifts are critical lines that are used to support and adjust the square sail yards. The upper three yards have *fixed lifts*. The lower topsail yards do not have any lifts. The courses have *adjustable lifts*.

1. Fixed lifts are used to give support to the yards. The upper three yards are movable and are hauled up or down when setting or dousing sail using the yard halyards and clewlines. When the sails are not set, the yards settle into their lifts. These lifts are

Figure 10. Gaff Topsail Detail

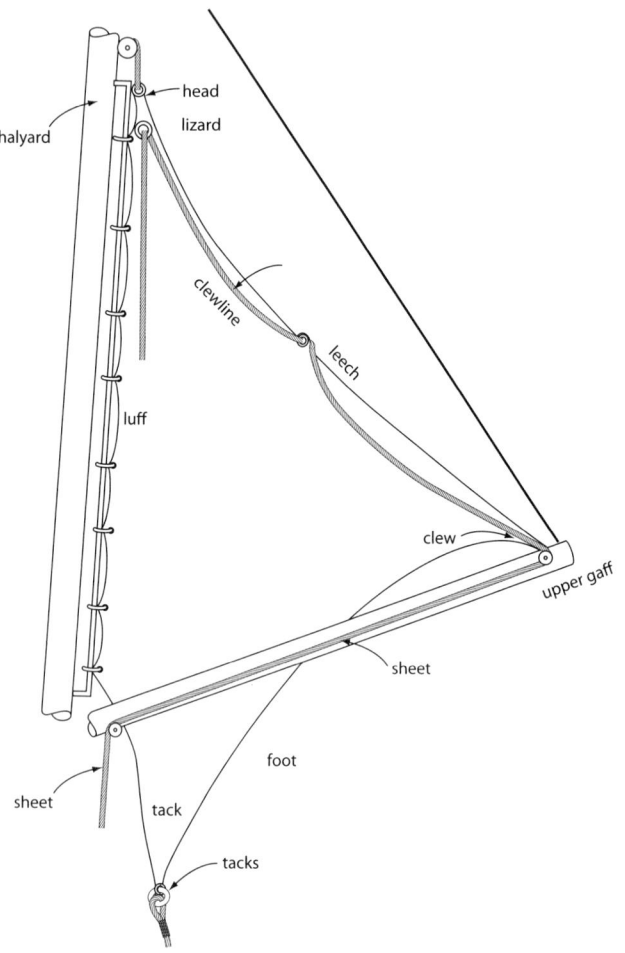

not adjustable. They support the yards and prevent them from working up and down. When a yard is lowered, care must be taken to ensure the fixed lifts become taut. Only then can personnel be assured the yard is in the lowered position, and not being held by the halyard.

When the sails are set, the yards are hauled up the mast and the fixed lifts hang slack. The leeches of the sails then tie the yards together, preventing the yards from working themselves up and down. When the sails are set, all of the yards can be trimmed at once with the course lifts.

2. The lower topsail yards do not have lifts since they are fixed on the mast and do not have halyards. When sails are doused, the lower topsail yards can be controlled by the upper topsail sheets.

3. The courses have adjustable lifts. A lift pendant leads from the yardarms to the mast and then back to the deck via a three-fold purchase. The lifts are adjustable so that *cockbill* may be removed and the yards can be trimmed parallel to the horizon, the optimum position for sailing.

As mentioned above, all of the yards are tied together when the sails are set, by the leeches of the sails. Sheets should be adjusted evenly on each side so that all five yards parallel each other and move together. Then, by adjusting the course lifts, all five yards will be trimmed simultaneously. The process of adjusting yards and removing cockbill is described in chapter 7.

Figure 11. Brace Detail

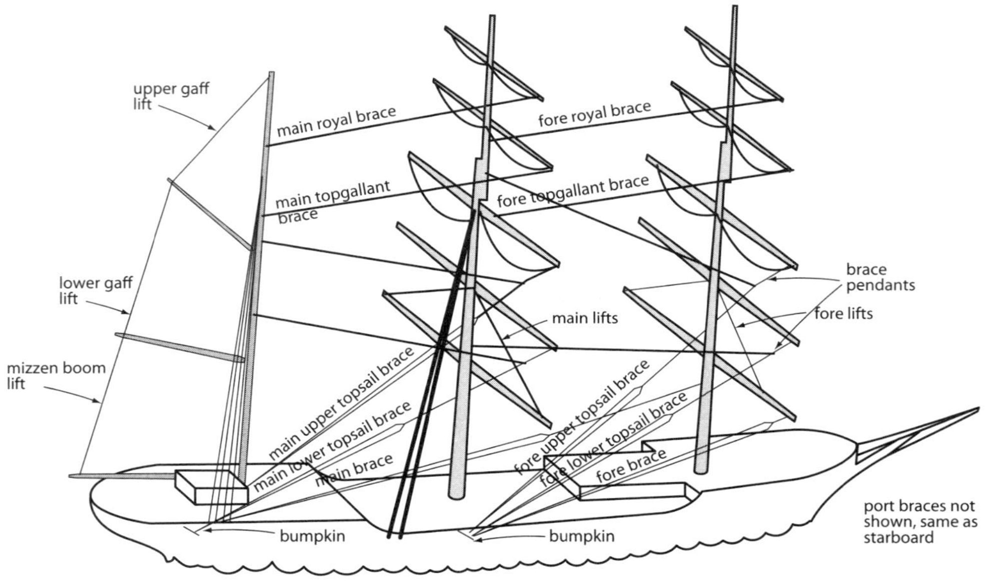

brace pendants

fore lifts

fore royal brace

fore topgallant brace

fore upper topsail brace

fore lower topsail brace

fore brace

bumpkin

main lifts

main royal brace

main topgallant brace

main upper topsail brace

main lower topsail brace

main brace

bumpkin

upper gaff lift

lower gaff lift

mizzen boom lift

port braces not shown, same as starboard

Braces

Braces adjust the fore-and-aft trim of the yards (see fig. 11). The braces for the lower three yards lead directly to the yard-arms from *bumpkins* on the sides of the barque. The upper two yards have braces that are led from the deck to the yardarms via a turning block high on the next mast aft. This arrangement results in a more horizontal lead for the topgallant and royal braces and makes their yards easier to control than the lower three yards. All braces are paired; whenever one brace is hauled, its companion on the opposite side must be eased.

The *timenoguy* is a special purchase, led from the mizzen shrouds, that is used to prevent the main braces from fouling on the boat davits when *bracing* the yards.

Location of Lines

By now it should be evident that there are more than a dozen types of running rigging on board *Eagle*. One of the most effective ways to learn the location of lines is to spend time on deck with "hands on."

Lines on deck are arranged logically so that it is easy to find any line once the location of a few key lines are learned. It is absolutely essential that all hands working the ship learn the lines since throwing off the wrong line can damage gear or seriously injure someone. For example, if the halyard for the upper topsail is thrown off by mistake, there is a good possibility that the topgallant square sail, which would have to bear the entire weight of the upper topsail yard and its gear, will tear. The tremendous weight of the yard as it slides down its track can also part the fixed lifts and result in the yard crashing to the deck.

Obviously, safe operation on board *Eagle* depends on all hands knowing the location and function of the lines.

The general rule for lines is that the higher the sail, the farther aft the line will be located. Except for halyards, downhauls, and the lines for the mizzensails and the gaff topsail, all lines are paired and are positioned directly opposite each other on the pinrails and fife rails.

Clewlines, buntlines, and bunt-leechlines for all square sails except the courses are grouped by sail on the pinrails. The sheets for these sails are located on the fife rails. All foresail and mainsail lines, except the tacks and sheets, are also located on the fife rails. The fore and main lifts, because they are threefold tackles, are easy to identify. The clew-garnets are immediately forward of the lifts; the remaining lines for the courses are immediately aft of the lifts.

Staysail downhauls are located on the after side of the fife rails. Headsail downhauls are located forward on the dograil. Headsail sheets lead to the *monkey rails* on the forecastle. The staysail sheets lead to the pinrails.

The halyards are grouped together. By locating the upper topsail halyard, it is easy to locate the remaining halyards on the fore and main. On both masts the upper topsail halyard has the largest line and the largest purchase. They are located on the port side on the fore and the starboard side on the main so that personnel setting the upper topsails will not interfere with each other when hauling on the halyards. The topgallant halyards are on the opposite pinrail, farther aft and with slightly smaller purchases. Finally, alternating again to the original side, are the royal halyards with the smallest purchases; they are farthest aft. Once the square sail halyards are learned, it is easy to locate the headsail and staysail halyards. Directly opposite the upper topsail halyards are the topmast staysail halyards. Opposite the main topgallant and royal halyards are the main topgallant staysail and royal staysail halyards, respectively. The headsail halyards alternate from starboard to port, the halyard for the higher sail being aft. Opposite, but slightly aft of the fore-topmast staysail halyard, is the inner jib halyard. The outer jib halyard is immediately aft of the fore-topmast staysail halyard. Finally, the flying jib halyard is immediately aft of the inner jib halyard. The halyards for the mizzen staysails and gaff topsail are located on the mizzen pinrails, except for the mizzen staysail halyard, which is on the mizzen fife rail. Lines for the upper and lower mizzensails, except for the sheets, are located on the mizzen fife rail.

The accompanying diagrams (figs. 12a–12f) should be studied to learn line locations. Lines can usually be identified by their size, lead, type, and position. For instance, all halyards have accompanying stoppers on deck to help belay them when under a strain. Again, if the functions of the lines are understood and the position of the most obvious lines memorized, it will be relatively easy to identify the remaining lines. To understand sailing *Eagle*, you must first learn the lines and their functions.

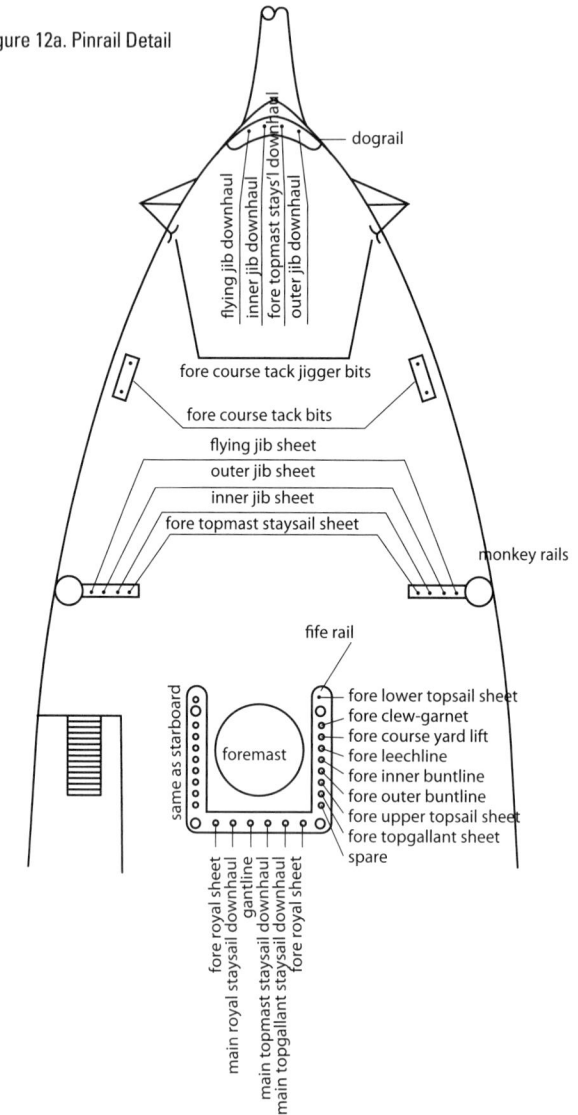

Figure 12a. Pinrail Detail

dograil

flying jib downhaul
inner jib downhaul
fore topmast stays'l downhaul
outer jib downhaul

fore course tack jigger bits

fore course tack bits

flying jib sheet

outer jib sheet

inner jib sheet

fore topmast staysail sheet

monkey rails

fife rail

same as starboard

foremast

fore lower topsail sheet
fore clew-garnet
fore course yard lift
fore leechline
fore inner buntline
fore outer buntline
fore upper topsail sheet
fore topgallant sheet
spare

fore royal sheet
main royal staysail downhaul
gantline
main topmast staysail downhaul
main topgallant staysail downhaul
fore royal sheet

Figure 12b. Pinrail Detail (continued)

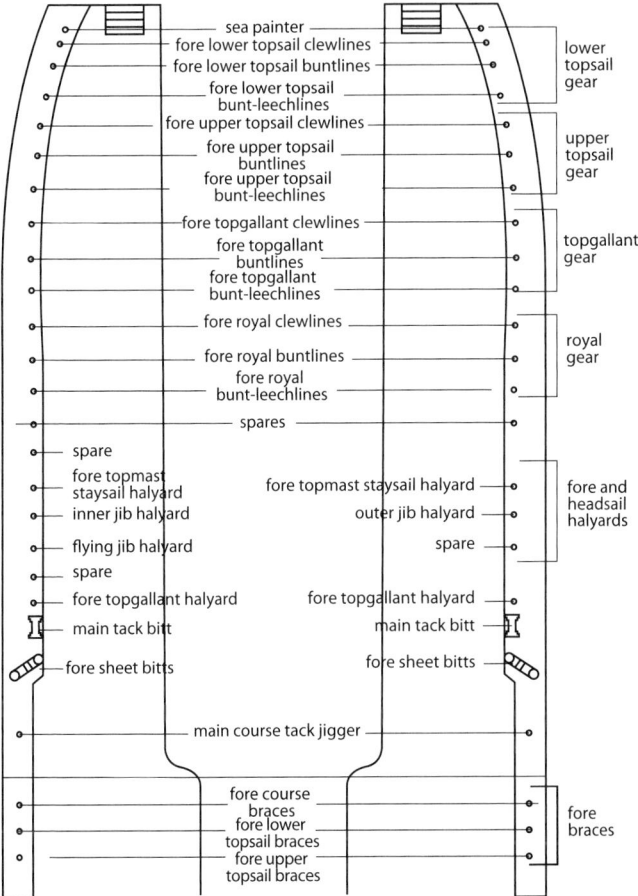

sea painter
fore lower topsail clewlines
fore lower topsail buntlines
fore lower topsail bunt-leechlines
fore upper topsail clewlines
fore upper topsail buntlines
fore upper topsail bunt-leechlines
fore topgallant clewlines
fore topgallant buntlines
fore topgallant bunt-leechlines
fore royal clewlines
fore royal buntlines
fore royal bunt-leechlines
spares

lower topsail gear

upper topsail gear

topgallant gear

royal gear

spare
fore topmast staysail halyard
inner jib halyard
flying jib halyard
spare
fore topgallant halyard
main tack bitt
fore sheet bitts

fore topmast staysail halyard
outer jib halyard
spare
fore topgallant halyard
main tack bitt
fore sheet bitts

fore and headsail halyards

main course tack jigger

fore course braces
fore lower topsail braces
fore upper topsail braces

fore braces

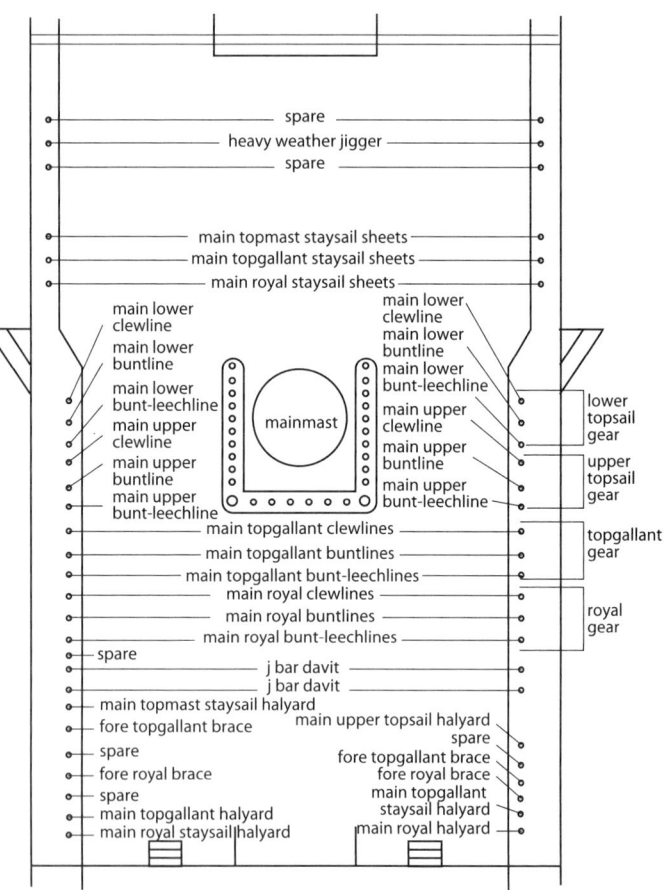

spare
heavy weather jigger
spare

main topmast staysail sheets
main topgallant staysail sheets
main royal staysail sheets

main lower clewline
main lower buntline
main lower bunt-leechline
main upper clewline
main upper buntline
main upper bunt-leechline

main lower clewline
main lower buntline
main lower bunt-leechline
main upper clewline
main upper buntline
main upper bunt-leechline

mainmast

lower topsail gear

upper topsail gear

main topgallant clewlines
main topgallant buntlines
main topgallant bunt-leechlines
main royal clewlines
main royal buntlines
main royal bunt-leechlines

topgallant gear

royal gear

spare
j bar davit
j bar davit
main topmast staysail halyard
fore topgallant brace
spare
fore royal brace
spare
main topgallant halyard
main royal staysail halyard

main upper topsail halyard
spare
fore topgallant brace
fore royal brace
main topgallant staysail halyard
main royal halyard

Figure 12d. Pinrail Detail (continued)

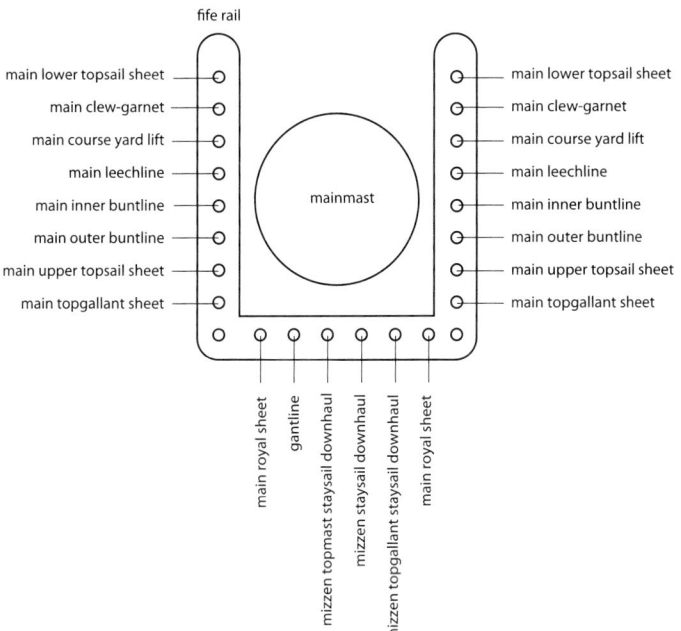

Figure 12e. Pinrail Detail (continued)

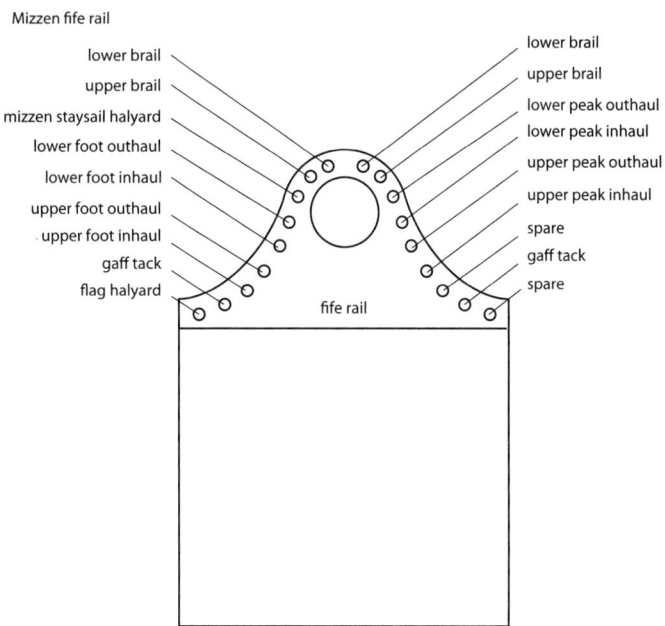

Mizzen fife rail

lower brail

upper brail

mizzen staysail halyard

lower foot outhaul

lower foot inhaul

upper foot outhaul

upper foot inhaul

gaff tack

flag halyard

fife rail

lower brail

upper brail

lower peak outhaul

lower peak inhaul

upper peak outhaul

upper peak inhaul

spare

gaff tack

spare

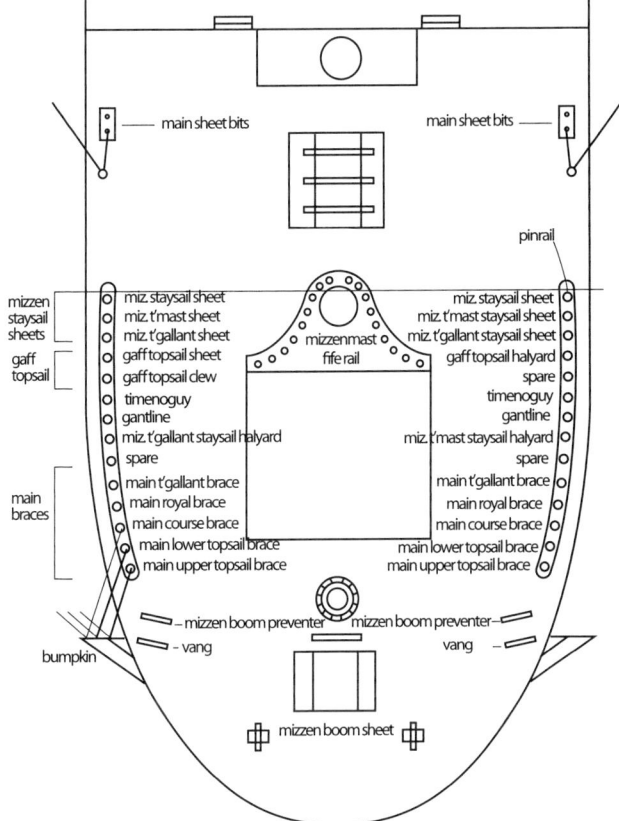

CHAPTER 5

Setting Sail

Sailing a square-rigger requires organization and teamwork to ensure that evolutions are safe and efficient. Because *Eagle* is a training vessel, this is particularly important. The failure of a single person to ease a line at the proper time can prevent the ship from tacking. Throwing off a line at the wrong time could potentially damage rigging or injure a shipmate. In no other setting is the need for a well-ordered chain of command so apparent. One of the most significant reasons for training on board a sailing ship is the opportunity trainees are given to organize and direct people into a close-knit team responsive to the orders of the commanding officer (CO). If any part fails, a ten-minute operation can easily grow into an hour of hard labor. The consequences of failing to organize properly and the great importance of every person in the chain of command are reinforced by the extra time and effort needed when an evolution fails. On the other hand, a well-prepared team will execute commands and evolutions easily; their teamwork and preparation will be readily apparent.

Organization

Trainees fill all sailing billets, from top to bottom in the chain of command. Each trainee in a supervisory position is supported by an officer or a petty officer who acts as the safety observer and technical adviser.

The chain of command for a sailing evolution starts with the trainee officer of the deck (OOD), who carries out the assigned sail evolution under the direct supervision of the officer of the deck and the commanding officer. The trainee OOD is responsible for the successful and safe completion of the evolution. The three trainee mast captains, supported by the permanent crew mast captains, report to the trainee OOD. The trainee mast captains must assign fellow upperclass trainees to act as supervisors in key positions. These positions depend upon the evolution but generally include someone in charge of each pinrail, fife rail, the braces, the headsails, and the staysails.

When problems arise, it is usually at this intermediate level of command. In most evolutions it is impossible for the mast captain to observe every line personally, so supervisors must learn to delegate. Yet without proper supervision, a minor problem with one line can easily become a major problem for the entire mast. The use of upperclass supervisors reduces the mast captain's span of control to a more manageable level of four or five personnel, allowing the mast captain to devote more attention to the evolution as a whole. In general these upperclass supervisors should remain at their stations throughout an evolution so they are always ready to respond to commands and direct the efforts of the underclass trainees.

Underclass trainees are an integral part of the chain of command, and are usually assigned to specific lines or yards by pinrail and fife rail captains. Each line captain is responsible for ensuring that the line is fully ready before reporting *"Manned and ready"* to her/his pinrail or fife rail captain. Specifically, the line captain must ensure that the line is properly faked out for running or led clear for hauling and that a sufficient number of personnel have manned the line to accomplish the task.

The number of personnel required on a given line usually depends upon wind and sea conditions, so the upperclass supervisors must intelligently gauge the conditions to assign the appropriate number of personnel. For example, assigning four or five trainees to ease a line with no strain on it is wasteful. Conversely, assigning one or two trainees to tend a staysail sheet in high winds can be very dangerous.

Although limited in experience, the underclass trainees are an essential part of the chain of command: the success or failure of the evolution often depends on the actions of these personnel. The underclass trainees must be well prepared and pay attention at all times so they do not miss a command or fail to understand a command given to another line or mast. Additionally, they must act as safety observers and report fouled lines and other problems to their pinrail or fife rail captain. Having a thorough knowledge of lines and commands is essential. Being well prepared makes all evolutions safer and easier to understand. It is also vital for the underclass trainees to learn all that they can since someday they will be in a supervisory role giving commands. Fundamental linehandling and seamanship skills are critical no matter what career path a future officer takes.

At the start of each cruise, when trainees are particularly unfamiliar with evolutions, it is important that the chain of command ensures that each supervisor's span of control is small enough to effectively monitor the assigned trainees. Later, the permanent crew at the intermediate supervisory levels can act as safety observers who give orders only by exception, such as stepping in if a line is improperly manned or if a problem develops. Leadership by exception is leadership in fact. This is typical of the organization of a cutter in a high-threat environment where the extra seconds used in passing commands down the chain make the difference between success and failure.

A well-ordered chain of command is absolutely essential for successful sailing evolutions. The normal trainee chain of command used is:

1. Trainee officer of the deck
2. Trainee mast captains
3. Pinrail and fife rail captains (upperclass)
4. Line captains (underclass)
5. Underclass trainees

The officer of the deck oversees all evolutions and reports directly to the commanding officer. The permanent crew mast captains are safety observers and work closely with the trainee mast captain and pinrail and fife rail captains as coaches and technical advisers.

Safety Aloft

Going to sea has always been inherently dangerous. Sailing a square-rigger can be particularly dangerous unless an attitude of safety consciousness is developed by each crew member and trainee. It is this vigilance, more than any specific rule or regulation, that ensures the safety of the vessel and her crew. It is critical before personnel lay aloft that their equipment is in working order, that they are mentally and physically prepared to work in the rig, and that they have been properly trained. What might be harmless horseplay ashore becomes potentially dangerous skylarking at sea. In short, safety at sea is a way of life.

Safety Rules for Working Aloft and On Deck

1. Take no unnecessary chances and never grandstand.

2. Always wear a safety harness when working above the deck. While actively moving up and down the shrouds, clips should be hooked into the belt so that they cannot foul, and standing rigging should be used for support whenever on yards, gaffs, or crane lines, and whenever stationary in the rig. Standing rigging includes jackstays, *safety stays*, shrouds, and crane lines; most standing rigging is painted black or white. Running rigging should never be used for support or for safety belts because it may become slack or may move. Likewise, belts should never be clipped into ratlines.

3. "One hand for the ship and one hand for yourself" is the rule, even when wearing a safety belt. Both feet should be on the ratlines, crane lines, footropes, or flemish horses at all times.

4. Always maintain at least three points of contact with standing rigging.

5. Hold onto the shrouds rather than the ratlines. Ratlines occasionally *carry away*, even with the best preventive maintenance.

6. Lay aloft only on the weather side. If a ratline carries away or you should lose your grip, the wind will blow you into the shrouds instead of overboard. This is particularly important as the ship heels.

7. Do not sit or stand on the yards. A sail in its gear may fly up and knock you off the yard.

8. In heavy winds, stay well clear of all headsail and staysail sheets. Parted sheets are extremely dangerous and can easily kill someone. Respect them!

9. Do not carry unnecessary gear aloft. Nametags, watches, hats, and the like must be left below. Gear that is carried aloft must be secured to personnel with a *lanyard*.

10. Do not lay out onto a yard unless it is securely in its fixed lifts or the sail is fully set, and the braces are taut.

11. When going aloft on the mizzen, make sure that all high-frequency (HF) radio transmitters in the combat information center (CIC), in the radio room, and on the bridge are secured.

12. While *unfurling*, the upper topsails should not be thrown in their gear until personnel have laid in from the lower topyards, to avoid the sails blowing into the faces of those working on the lower topyard.

13. On deck, personnel assigned to headsail and staysail sheets must be particularly careful to control the sheets when setting and dousing. The blocks on the headsail sheets (known as "widow makers" for their ability to seriously injure personnel) may easily gyrate and hit someone if not attended to diligently and controlled carefully. The mizzen staysail sheets are particularly dangerous because of their close proximity to bridge personnel who may be focused on other tasks.

14. When handling lines, a sufficient number of personnel must be assigned according to wind conditions. Bad rope burns can easily occur if a line is undermanned, not to mention the potential damage to the gear.

15. Keep hands away from blocks when hauling lines and stand clear of bights. Lines can run so fast that a foot or an arm can be caught without warning in the block or a bight (loop in a line). Never straddle a line.

16. In all shipboard evolutions, and especially during sailing evolutions, silence must be maintained except for necessary commands and reports.

17. While on the bowsprit, never work on the *leeward* side of a headsail as a sudden gust can easily knock a person overboard.

Overshadowing these individual safety rules are forehand-edness and common sense—traits possessed by all good mariners and absolute necessities for an officer standing watch. All hands must anticipate potential safety problems and take action to avoid them. Only through a forehanded appreciation of the inherent dangers of sailing and a strong spirit of safety consciousness can serious accidents be avoided. Safety is never to be sacrificed in favor of saving time or for convenience.

Setting Sail

Although almost all of the 190 lines on board are used when setting and dousing sail, the process is actually quite straight-forward. A good crew can set all sail in less than fifteen minutes and take in all sail in less than five. In contrast, an inexperienced crew may take well over an hour to set or douse.

The traditional order for setting square sails is from the bottom up, although the courses are normally set after the topsails. Topsails are traditional maneuvering or fighting sails. They are located higher on the mast and are therefore exposed to steadier wind when working the ship in tight quarters. *Eagle* has split topsails: a lower topsail bent to a fixed yard and an upper topsail bent to a movable yard. Courses are large sails that provide a majority of the ship's driving speed, but they are awkward to handle and reduce the visibility of the conning officer. They are set after the topsails, and only in open water. Royal and topgallant sails are "light-air" sails, used for maximizing ship speed in lighter wind conditions. Thus, the order usually followed is:

1. Lower topsails
2. Upper topsails
3. Courses
4. Topgallants
5. Royals

Headsails and staysails are similarly set from the lowest to the highest. The mizzen staysail, however, is frequently not set because of its close proximity to the exhaust stack.

With all hands at sail stations, it is possible to set sail in unison; that is, the matched square sails on the foremast and mainmast are set at the same time, along with the corresponding headsails, staysails, and mizzensails. These roughly horizontal tiers of sails maintain sail balance by keeping the sails' center of effort just aft of *Eagle*'s pivot point, avoiding excessive *weather helm*. Sail balance is discussed in detail in chapter 7.

Sails are doused in reverse order. This order of setting and dousing reflects the natural order of taking in sails as winds increase. Royals, topgallants, and upper staysails are normally taken in first, since they heel the ship excessively in high winds without adding significantly to *Eagle*'s speed. Courses are taken in before topsails because of their large size and the relative difficulty in handling them. In light winds all staysails or headsails may be set or doused at the same time.

Unfurling

Before sails can be set, they must be unfurled. When furled, sails are secured to *Eagle*'s spars with sailcloth straps called *gaskets*. When the OOD gives the order to set sail, the mast captain will give the command *"Lay aloft and loose all (or a given) sail."* Before personnel actually lay aloft, the mast captain must ensure that the braces are taut and that the upper yards are in their fixed lifts. The mast captain should also ensure that all clewlines, buntlines, bunt-leechlines, and leechlines are taut. If not, the sail may belly out when the gaskets are loosened, which may knock a person from the yard or damage gear. With an inexperienced crew or when in a moderate breeze, a yard captain should be assigned to supervise the unfurling aloft. On the command *"Let fall,"* a square sail is pushed off the forward side of the yard; it is then *in its gear*. This command may be given by the mast captain, or it may be delegated to the yard captain. After the sail is in its gear, personnel lay in to the mast.

In light winds two people on each yard are sufficient to unfurl sail. They should start at the yardarm and throw off gaskets as they work their way inboard to the mast. This procedure cannot be used in strong winds since the sail may belly out before all of the gaskets are clear and may jam the remaining gaskets. Moreover, with a single person on each yard, the sail will not be put into its gear all at once; it will slat about and possibly tear. Therefore, when in strong winds or when time is critical, four to six personnel should be sent to each yard so that the entire sail can be thrown into its gear at the same time. The lower yards obviously require more people since the sails are much larger.

When setting sail with only the watch on deck, trainees must lay aloft, unfurl sail, and then lay down to the deck to assist with linehandling. However, during all-hands sail evolutions, sails will often be quickly put in their gear in order. In this case, eight personnel typically will lay aloft on each square-rigged mast. All eight personnel will unfurl and let fall the lower topsail. Next, the group will split: four personnel will lay in and up to loose the topgallant and royal gear, while the remaining four personnel lay in to loose the upper topsail and course gear. After unfurling sail, personnel remain in the tops or trees to *overhaul* gear once it is set. Depending on the sail configuration, some variation of this technique can save a significant amount of time during all-hands evolutions.

Setting Staysails and Headsails

Staysails and headsails are easier to set than the square sails. They are potentially much more dangerous, however, because of the whipping sheet blocks on the headsails aptly called "widow makers." Staysail sheets are normally not rigged when the sails are furled. Thus, the first step in setting staysails is to rig the sheet to the sheet pendant and to put the sail into its gear.

Particular care must be taken in rigging sheets since an error can easily result in a torn sail, even in moderate winds. Sheets must be led outboard of the stays and clear of the *gant-lines* and other lines leading down the after side of the mast. The sheet for a staysail is always rigged aft and outboard of the staysail below it. Headsail sheets are permanently rigged and are therefore always ready for setting.

For setting, the downhaul is faked out for running, the sheet is tended, and the halyard is hauled until the luff of the sail is taut and no *scallops* are seen. Normally at least four or five personnel are needed on a halyard, although in high winds, twice that number will be needed. If enough people are available, all headsails or staysails on a mast can be set simultaneously. As the sail is hauled up, the sheet is tended; once the halyard is belayed, the sheet is sheeted home to its final position, trimming the sail for maximum efficiency. If the sheet is too tight when setting a headsail or staysail, it will bind the hanks against the stay and make it difficult to set the sail; if the sheets are excessively slack, the widow makers will slat about and may tear the sail or injure someone.

If there are not enough personnel available to man the sheets and halyard simultaneously, the sheets may be made off at an intermediate strain while the sail is raised. After all scallops are removed and the halyard is made off, personnel may then trim the sail using the sheet for maximum efficiency. In high winds, it may be necessary to use a *rattail jigger* to sweat the sheet home.

Sail trim is discussed in chapter 7. The sails must be trimmed, however, so the sheet of an upper sail does not chafe against a lower sail; such chafing will quickly wear through the sail. Staysails are frequently trimmed in too far. Sheeting the staysails flat will not necessarily result in more driving power, and a fore-and-aft sail that is trimmed in too far will actually stall and result in more *leeway* than driving power. For proper trim, the sheets are eased until the sail luffs and then sheeted in just to the point where the sail draws again. Also, the wire rope pendant of the weather sheet on the headsails (which does not have any strain) will quickly chafe through if it is allowed to lay on the forestays. Thus, after the headsails are set, the weather headsail sheet pendants and their blocks should be passed over the stays. As a result, the synthetic sheet itself, which can more easily stand the chafing, will lie on the stay.

Fore-and-aft sail sheets tend to gyrate if they are not carefully controlled when the sail is being set or doused. As a result, everyone should stand well clear of the staysail sheets (and headsail sheet blocks) when setting or dousing.

The commands for setting any headsail or staysail are given in the following sequence.

1. Mast captain (once all lines have reported manned and ready): *"On the main-topmast staysail (flying jib, etc.). Ease the downhaul. Tend the sheet. Haul around on the halyard."*

2. Mast captain (when the sail is almost set): *"Hand over hand the halyard."*

3. Mast captain (when all scallops are removed from the luff): *"That's well. Belay."* The pinrail captain will then properly trim the sail by the sheet without further command.

In complex evolutions such as tacking, the mast captain may delegate the setting of the staysails to an upperclass pinrail or fife rail captain, in which case the mast captain will give just the command *"Set the staysails or headsails,"* and the rail captain will give the rest of the commands.

Setting Square Sails

Generally speaking, it takes one step to set the lowest two square sails, and two steps to set the upper three square sails. The first step (the only step for the courses and lower topsails) is to *"Sheet home,"* hauling the sail down to the next lower yard (to the deck for the courses). The second step is to *"Haul around on the halyard,"* raising the movable yard until the sail's leeches are taut.

For the topsails, topgallants, and royals, sheeting home involves hauling on the sheets and easing the clewlines, buntlines, and bunt-leechlines. They should be tended and not just thrown off, to ensure that they run freely and do not jam. In sheeting home, the clew of the sail should not be hauled down into the cheek block of the lower yard since it may jam. Several links of the sheet chain should remain visible when the sail is properly set. An equal amount of sheet chain should be showing on each side to allow the adjustable lifts to trim all five yards together.

The courses are a different matter, since they are the largest sails. On the command *"Sheet home,"* the course tacks and sheets are hauled, as appropriate, and the clew-garnets, inner and outer buntlines, and leechlines are eased. Wind conditions will dictate the appropriate manning levels for the course tacks, and personnel may require the assistance of a *stopper* to properly belay the line.

Appropriate manning of course tacks and sheets is also dependent upon *Eagle*'s point of sail. When braced sharp, all of the strain will be on the weather tack and the *lee* sheet, and individual personnel can handle the remaining tack and sheet. When braced square, both sheets will have to be manned equally, with a single person tending each tack. When braced anywhere in between, personnel should be stationed as necessary according to the conditions.

Whenever the yards are braced three points or sharp, the command *"Board the tack"* should be given. The tack jigger is used to haul the weather leech taut to ensure proper airflow across the leading edge of the sail. When the tack is boarded, the weather clew will lie forward of the yardarm and the leeward clew will lie aft of the leeward yardarm. With the wind abaft the beam, the tack is normally not boarded.

Figure 13. Setting a Square Sail

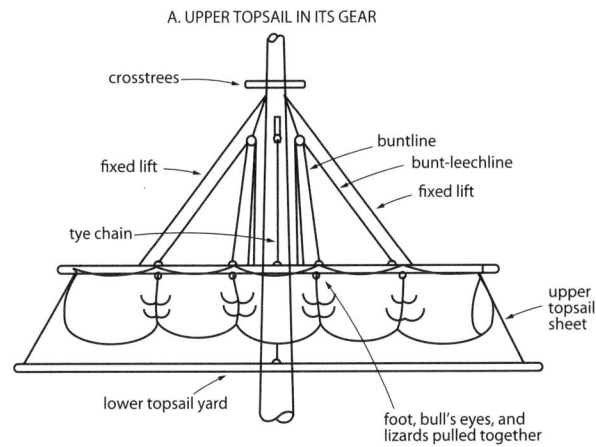

A. UPPER TOPSAIL IN ITS GEAR

crosstrees

fixed lift

buntline
bunt-leechline
fixed lift

tye chain

upper topsail sheet

lower topsail yard

foot, bull's eyes, and lizards pulled together

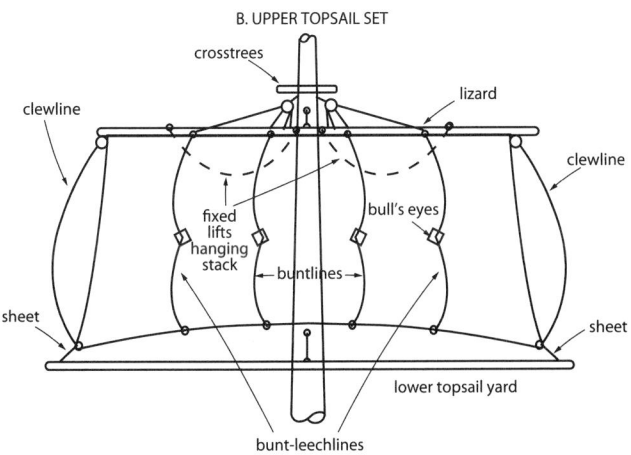

B. UPPER TOPSAIL SET

crosstrees

clewline

lizard

clewline

fixed lifts hanging stack

bull's eyes

buntlines

sheet

sheet

lower topsail yard

bunt-leechlines

The commands for setting the lower topsail or course are given in the following sequence.

1. Manning (once the sail is in its gear):
   a. Mast captain: *"Man the lower topsail gear."* Trainees will man the clewlines, buntlines, and bunt-leechlines. Normally the first trainee to reach a line becomes the line captain, in charge of that line. When the line is rigged for running and is properly manned, the line captain will report to the supervisor, *"Line manned and ready."*

2. Setting:
   a. Mast captain: "On the lower topsail. Sheet home."
   b. Pinrail line captains: *"Ease the clewlines, buntlines, and bunt-leechlines."*
   c. Sheet line captain: *"Haul around on the sheets."*
   d. Mast captain: "That's well. Belay."

The other square sails are set similarly to this point. The courses are slightly different. When the mast captain gives the command *"Sheet home,"* the pinrail captains designate which lines shall be worked, such as *"Haul around on the weather tack and tend the lee sheet."*

To complete setting the upper three square sails, the yard to which the sail is bent must be raised into position. This is accomplished by hauling around on the halyard while continuing to ease the clewlines, buntlines, and bunt-leechlines.

When raising a yard, it is also critical to ensure that the sheets for the sail above have been thrown off, so that the sheet does not bind as the yard moves up. Depending on how the yards are braced, the angles involved in the sheet leads vary. The leads of the sheets are geometrically complex, making it hard to predict which sheet will become taut at a given point of sail. Therefore, it is best to throw them both off when raising and lowering a yard to prevent the sheets from binding and possibly parting. Since the sail above the moving yard will not be set at this time, there is no strain on the sheets, and there is no danger in throwing them off.

Figure 14. Easing Brace for Setting Square Sails

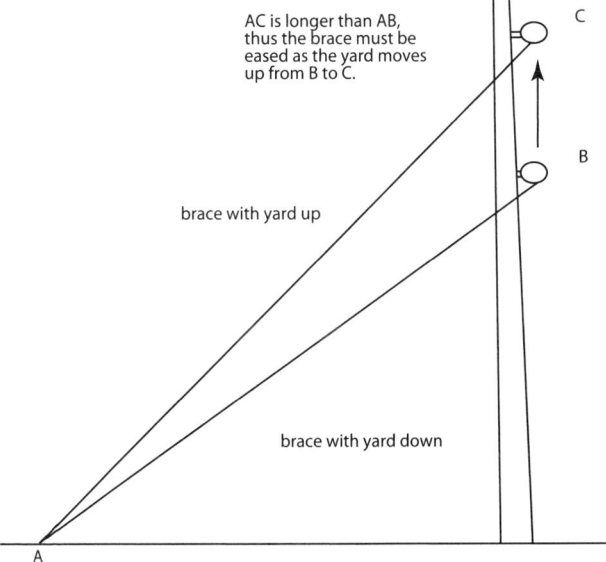

Upper topsail braces

AC is longer than AB, thus the brace must be eased as the yard moves up from B to C.

C

B

brace with yard up

brace with yard down

A

Figure 15. Geometry of Square Sail Sheets

Sheets for a movable yard

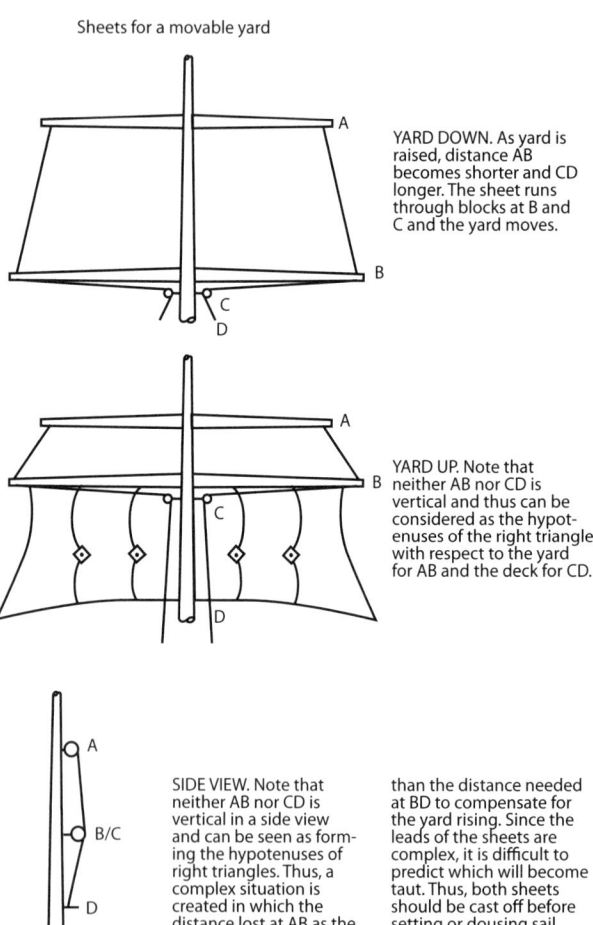

YARD DOWN. As yard is raised, distance AB becomes shorter and CD longer. The sheet runs through blocks at B and C and the yard moves.

YARD UP. Note that neither AB nor CD is vertical and thus can be considered as the hypotenuses of the right triangles with respect to the yard for AB and the deck for CD.

SIDE VIEW. Note that neither AB nor CD is vertical in a side view and can be seen as forming the hypotenuses of right triangles. Thus, a complex situation is created in which the distance lost at AB as the yard rises may be less than the distance needed at BD to compensate for the yard rising. Since the leads of the sheets are complex, it is difficult to predict which will become taut. Thus, both sheets should be cast off before setting or dousing sail.

Additionally, it is necessary to ease the braces for each movable yard to allow the yard to travel freely up its track. Failing to ease the braces will result in a parted brace or a bent yard. For the topgallant and royal yards, it is only necessary to ease the lee brace as the yard moves up.

Once the sheets to the sail above have been thrown off and the braces are ready to be eased, setting the upper square sails is simple. The halyard is hauled until the leeches are taut.

The commands for setting the upper three square sails are given in the following sequence.

1. Manning and sheeting home are completed in the same fashion as with the lower topsail. After all stations are manned and ready, the sheets for the sail above have been thrown off, and the braces are ready to be eased, the following commands are given:

   a. Mast captain to supervisors: *"On the main topgallant (royal, etc.). Sheet home."*

   b. Pinrail line captains: *"Ease the clewlines, buntlines, and bunt-leechlines."*

   c. Sheet line captain: *"Haul around on the sheets."*

   d. Mast captain: *"That's well. Belay."*

2. Raising the yard:

   a. Mast captain: *"On the main topgallant (royal, etc.). Haul around on the halyard."* An upperclass supervisor should relay the command and then stand near the halyard to act as a safety observer. Clewlines, buntlines, and bunt-leechlines are eased. On the upper topsail, especially when raising both the fore and main upper topsails together, it is often easier to *"Walk away with the halyard."* This involves walking forward with the main upper topsail halyard and aft with the fore upper topsail. Personnel who are hauling may move in a counterclockwise rotation around the *waist* and through the galley serving line to maximize efficiency.

b. Brace line captains: *"Ease the lee topgallant (or royal) brace"* or *"Ease the upper topsail braces."* The brace captain should order the personnel on the braces to ease the braces enough so that the yard can go up easily but not enough to allow the yard to swing out of control. The brace captain should also adjust the braces to provide an appropriate fan. The weather brace is not eased on the royals and topgallants and should not be eased much on the upper topsail. If it is eased too much it may take up to a dozen people to haul against the force of the wind and correct the mistake of a single person. Not easing the brace enough, however, can cause binding or, even worse, may lead to a yard being bent. Obviously the brace captain plays a critical role in setting or dousing sail.

c. Mast captain (when sail is almost set): *"Hand over hand the halyard."*

d. Mast captain (when the leeches draw taut): *"That's well. Pass the stopper. Belay."* A stopper is always passed to belay the square sail halyards.

After square sails are set it may be necessary to overhaul the gear. The weight of the buntlines and bunt-leechlines, especially in light air, may curl the foot of the sail. When overhauling, topmen should pull excess line aloft through the lizards so that there is slack in the buntlines, bunt-leechlines, and leechlines, allowing the sail to draw properly. These lines are then firmly tucked under the jackstays to keep the strain off the foot of the sail, while still ensuring that the lines can be pulled free if hauled on from the deck.

Setting the Lower and Upper Mizzensails

Setting the lower and upper mizzensails is quite easy. The preventer must first be rigged on the leeward side. The boom is then positioned for sail setting by hauling on the preventer while easing the sheet and weather vang, and tending the flag halyard. Unless the ship is rolling heavily, three or four personnel will normally suffice on the preventer and one each on the remaining lines. Once the boom is positioned, the sail is set by hauling on the outhauls while easing the inhauls and brails.

Since the lower and upper mizzensails are two of the largest sails, several people are needed to set them. A single person can handle all of the brails on one side; similarly, one person is sufficient for each inhaul. At least four personnel each should be stationed on the peak and foot outhauls.

The commands for setting the mizzensails are given in the following sequence.

1. Preliminary steps:
   a. Mast captain: *"Man the mizzen boom gear. Rig the preventer."*
   b. Mast captain: *"Ease the sheet. Tend the vangs and flag halyard. Haul around on the preventer. That's well. Belay."*
   c. Mast captain: *"Man the lower mizzen (upper mizzen) gear."*

2. Setting the sail (after it is ungasketed):
   a. Mast captain: *"Ease the inhauls and the brails. Haul around on the outhauls."*

b. Mast captain (when all scallops have been removed from the head and foot): *"That's well. Belay the lower mizzen gear."*

Setting the Gaff Topsail

The gaff topsail is set much like a staysail. The halyard hauls the sail up and the sheet hauls the clew out to the end of the gaff. The clewline, like a downhaul, is eased. The tack is tended and then used to trim the luff and foot of the sail after the halyard and sheet have been belayed. Three or four people are sufficient for the halyard and sheet; a single person can handle the clewline and another the tack.

The commands for setting the gaff topsail are given in the following sequence.

Mast captain: *"On the gaff topsail. Ease the clewline. Tend the tack. Haul around on the halyard. That's well. Belay. Sheet home. That's well. Belay."*

It should be noted that in giving commands for setting sails, the commands *"Ease"* and *"Tend"* are always given before the command *"Haul"* on any line. This is because almost every line is opposed by another, and before you can haul on one line another must be eased. Otherwise, gear may tear or lines may part.

CHAPTER 6

Shortening Sail and Harbor Preparations

Shortening Sail

Using the proper terminology for shortening sail: headsails, staysails, and the gaff topsail are *doused*; square sails are *taken in*; and the mizzensails are *brailed in*.

Dousing Headsails and Staysails

The headsails and staysails are doused by easing the halyard, tending the sheet, and hauling around on the downhaul. The sheets must be handled carefully. If slacked, the sail will slat about and perhaps tear, and the sheet blocks will whip around dangerously. On the other hand, if the sheets are too taut, it will be difficult to haul the sail down, since the hanks will bind to the stay. The downhaul runs from the fife rail to the head of the sail and then to the clew.

In dousing, therefore, the sheet should be held until the head of the sail is hauled down to the miter seam. Holding the sheet allows the sheet to oppose the downhaul so that the head of the sail can be hauled down to the miter seam and collapse the top half of the sail. Then the sheet should be eased to allow the sail to be completely doused.

Obviously, careful coordination between the pinrail and fife rail captains is needed throughout the operation. If enough personnel are available, all staysails on a mast may be doused at once. Whenever handling the main-topmast staysail, the mainmast captain should station sail handlers on the boat deck to ensure that it does not tear on the accommodation ladder or brows.

The commands for dousing any headsail or staysail are given in the following sequence.

> Mast captain: *"On the fore-topmast staysail (main royal staysail, etc.). Ease the halyard. Tend the sheet. Haul around on the downhaul. That's well. Belay."*

Taking in Square Sails

The procedure for taking in a square sail is the reverse of that for setting it: those lines that were hauled during setting are eased, and those lines that were eased are now hauled. The first step for the upper three square sails is to ease the halyard to bring the yard down into its fixed lifts and spill most of the wind from the sail.

It might appear that the great weight of the yards and their sails would bring them down easily when the halyard is eased, but this is sometimes not the case. The entire force of the wind on the sail is concentrated on the yard *shoe*, which rides on a track on the forward side of the mast. This tremendous pressure, even in moderate winds, often binds the shoe against the track and resists the yard being lowered. Thus, it is necessary to haul the yard down using the only available lines, the clewlines. On the command *"Clew down,"* the sheets remain belayed, the halyard is eased, and the clewlines are hauled. The sheets for the sail above are thrown off to prevent any possible binding, and the braces, which were eased in setting, are rounded in.

When slack develops in the halyard and the yard appears to be down, it is critical for the mast captain to glance aloft and ensure that the yard is actually sitting in its fixed lifts prior to continuing the evolution.

When the yard is securely in its lifts, the sail is hauled up into its gear. On the command *"Clew up,"* sheets are eased, and clewlines, buntlines, and bunt-leechlines are hauled until the sail is gathered up to the yard. On the courses, the process is the same, except that tacks must also be eased. On the courses, the command is *"Rise tacks and sheets."* The lower topsail, which is bent to a fixed yard, is taken in by merely clewing up.

The commands for taking in a square sail are given in the following sequence.

1. Preparatory steps:
    a. Fake the halyard and sheets free for running, since a jam could result in the sail slatting about violently and possibly tearing.
    b. Throw off the sheets for the sail above (movable yards only).
    c. Clear away the tack jigger (courses only).

2. Lowering the yards (upper three sails):
    a. Mast captain: *"Clew down."*
    b. Pinrail line captains: *"Ease the halyard"* or *"Haul around on the clewlines,"* as appropriate. Buntlines and bunt-leechlines are tended as the yard comes down. Those easing the halyard must keep at least a half round turn on the pin to keep the halyard from running out of control and the yard from crashing down into its lifts.
    c. Brace captain: *"Round in the lee brace"* (both braces on the upper topsail). For the topgallants and royals, rounding in just the lee brace and leaving the weather brace belayed will make resetting sail simple. If the yards were

properly fanned before they were lowered, they will be fanned again when the sails are reset if only the lee brace has been handled.

3. Taking in the sail:

   a. Mast captain: *"On the fore royal (topgallant, etc.). Clew up."* This command should be given as soon as the lifts come taut and the line captain on the halyard sounds off *"Slack in the halyard."* Ideally the people on the clewlines will continue hauling as the sheets are eased, although with an inexperienced crew this may not be possible.

   Since the lower topsails have no halyard, *"Clew up"* is the only command necessary. For the courses, *"Rise tacks and sheets"* is the proper command, and the clew-garnets are hauled instead of clewlines.

   b. Fife rail captain: *"On the fore royal. Ease the sheets."* Line captains must ease the sheets in a lively fashion since one person holding a sheet can easily check a half dozen hauling on the clewlines.

   c. Pinrail captain: *"On the fore royal. Haul around on the clewlines, buntlines, and bunt-leechlines."* The pinrail captains must carefully monitor the dousing of the sail and be prepared to order *"That's well"* on each line as the sail is hauled up to the yard. The lines usually come up at different rates and hauling on a line when the sail is already in its gear may tear out a bull's eye or jam a clew block. The mast captain is generally a safety observer and also ensures that no lines are being hauled after they are *two-blocked* and makes sure that no lines jam.

Brailing in the Lower and Upper Mizzensails

Brailing in the lower or upper mizzen is much like clewing up on a square sail: outhauls are eased, inhauls and brails are hauled. After the sail is brailed in the boom is centered by hauling on the sheet and easing the preventer. The preventer is then struck.

The commands for brailing in the mizzensails are given in the following sequence.

1. Braling in:
   a. Mast captain: *"On the lower mizzen (upper mizzen). Ease the outhauls. Haul around on the inhauls and brails. That's well. Belay."*

2. Securing:
   a. Mast captain: *"On the mizzen boom. Ease the preventer. Tend the vangs and flag halyard. Haul around on the sheet."*
   b. Mast captain (when the boom and gaffs are amidships): *"That's well. Belay."*

Dousing the Gaff Topsail

The gaff topsail is doused much like a staysail. The halyard and sheet are eased and the clewline hauled. The tack usually has little strain on it and can be left untended.

The commands for dousing the gaff topsail are given in the following sequence.

Mast captain: *"On the gaff topsail. Ease the halyard and sheet. Haul around on the clewline. That's well. Belay."*

Furling Sail

In very light air, it is permissible to leave the sails in their gear without furling. In stronger winds, the sails will slat about and quickly chafe; thus, they must be furled. There are two types of furls: the *sea furl* is used when rapid furling is required and appearance is not a factor; the *harbor furl* is far more time consuming and produces the sharpest appearance for events in port.

Sea Furling Square Sails

Furling is an art more easily learned from practice than described in a text. Figures 16a–16f illustrate the proper way to furl a square sail. In heavy winds, when there is danger of the sail slatting about, personnel should be stationed in the crosstrees and tops so they may immediately lay out onto the yards when the sails are up in their gear. Under such conditions, the weather side of the sail must be smothered first so gusts cannot catch the weather leech and cause the sail to belly out of the hands of the people who are trying to furl it.

To achieve a tight furl, the sail must be completely clewed up to the yard. Care must be taken to neither jam a clew in the clew block nor to pull the lizards for the buntlines and buntleechlines above the yard, where they will impede furling. The leech of the sail should be brought up parallel to the yard and held there until the last bight is dropped in, in case an awkward tangle of sail is created at the leeches.

In furling, an arm's-length bight of sail is taken simultaneously by all people on the yard. It is pulled up and held against the yard. As subsequent bights are taken, the earlier ones are dropped into it, until the entire sail has been taken up and the last few feet of the sail (at the head) form a tight skin. The entire sail is then rolled up onto the yard and set between the jackstay

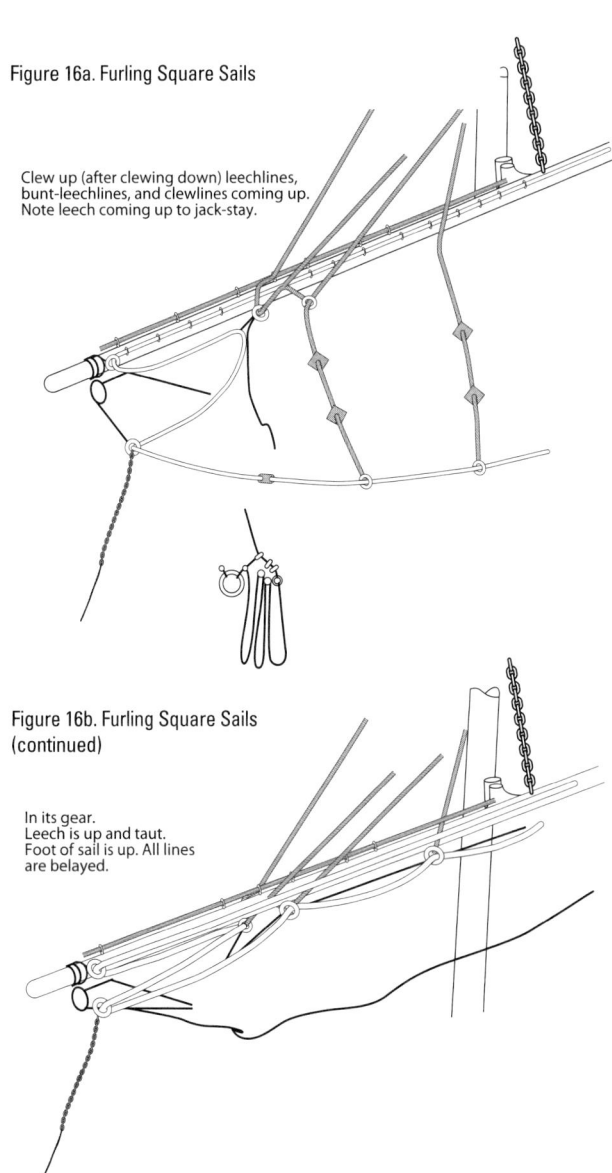

Figure 16a. Furling Square Sails

Clew up (after clewing down) leechlines, bunt-leechlines, and clewlines coming up. Note leech coming up to jack-stay.

Figure 16b. Furling Square Sails (continued)

In its gear.
Leech is up and taut.
Foot of sail is up. All lines are belayed.

Figure 16c. Furling Square Sails (continued)

Yard manned. Note furlers keeping leech up on yard. Foot pulled up to yard.

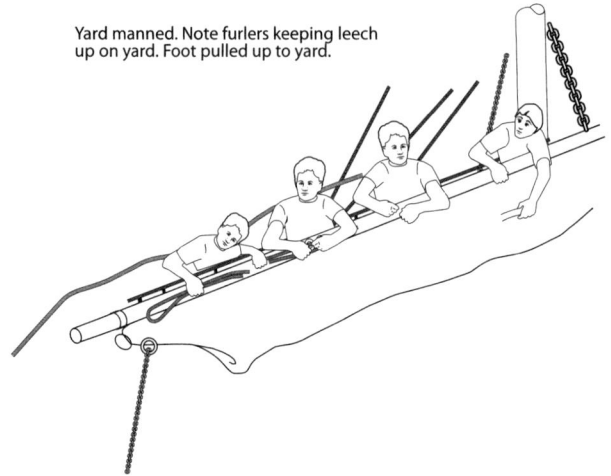

Figure 16d. Furling Square Sails (continued)

Furling. Furlers must keep together, lifting each bight uniformly. Outboard furler continues to keep leech up on the yard.

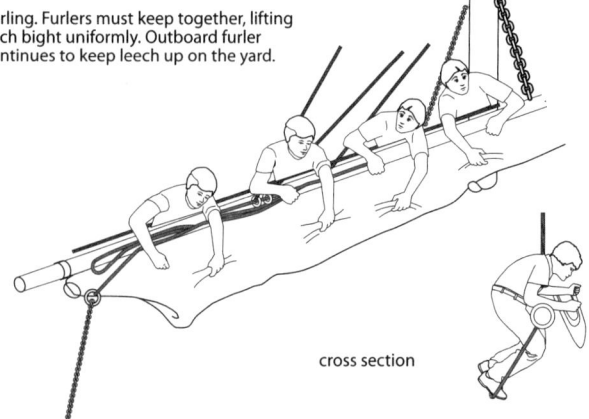

cross section

Sail almost furled. Drop each bight into the following bight until a tight skin is attained. Drop leech and foot just before the last bight is taken. Roll sail up on yard.

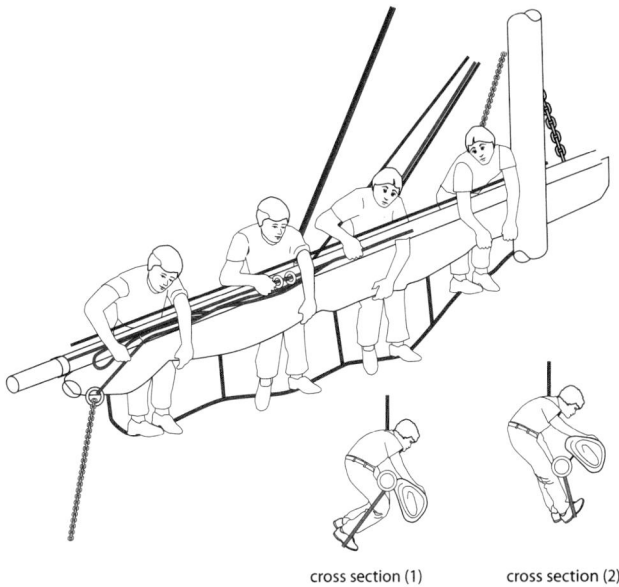

cross section (1)   cross section (2)

Figure 16f. Furling Square Sails (continued)

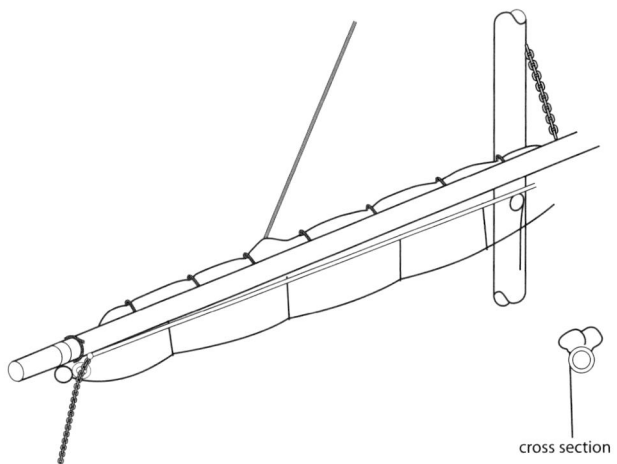

Sail furled. Note that sail is wrinkle free and lying flat between jackstay and safety stay. Buntlines and leechline stopped off near mast.

cross section

and the safety stay. Gaskets should then be passed over the sail and secured to the safety stay with a slip clove hitch. Care must be taken to ensure that there are no *deadmen* and that gaskets are snug to prevent the sail from working loose.

Harbor Furling Square Sails

When appearance is important (as when entering port), sails are usually harbor furled. The process is basically the same as sea furling but is more time consuming. The clew of the sail is brought up tight and the leech held against the yard. The foot of the sail, however, is held against the yard and the buntlines eased out so that the sail hangs in a single large bight. Forearm-length bights are then taken and held, layer by layer, against the yard. The final bight is drawn tightly over the rest of the sail to form a smooth skin and the sail is pulled up on top of the yard. After the sail has been furled, buntlines and leechlines may be stopped off to the mast to give a neater appearance.

Proper harbor furling requires near-calm conditions and close coordination. It is best to assign a yard captain to coordinate the taking of the bights. A good harbor furl will be perfectly smooth and will not be seen from on deck aft of the mast.

Sea Furling Fore-and-Aft Sails

All fore-and-aft sails are furled in basically the same way. Topmen should lay out on the crane lines on either side of the sail and furl the sail into itself until it is tight enough for gaskets to be passed and until the remaining sail material can form a protective skin around the rest of the sail. Gaskets are then passed around the sail.

Although two people can sea furl a fore-and-aft sail, the process is much easier if one person is stationed on each crane line so the whole sail can be furled simultaneously. Headsails are furled in much the same way, but gaskets are passed over the bowsprit.

Harbor Furling Headsails and Staysails

In harbor furling a staysail, the first step is to shake the sail out so that it hangs freely. Then locate the miter seam—it runs from the clew to the center of the luff. The seam must be positioned vertically along the after side of the sail. The body of the sail is then tightly rolled inward from either side. When furled, the miter seam is still vertical and directly aft, and the entire sail

Figure 17. Furling Staysails

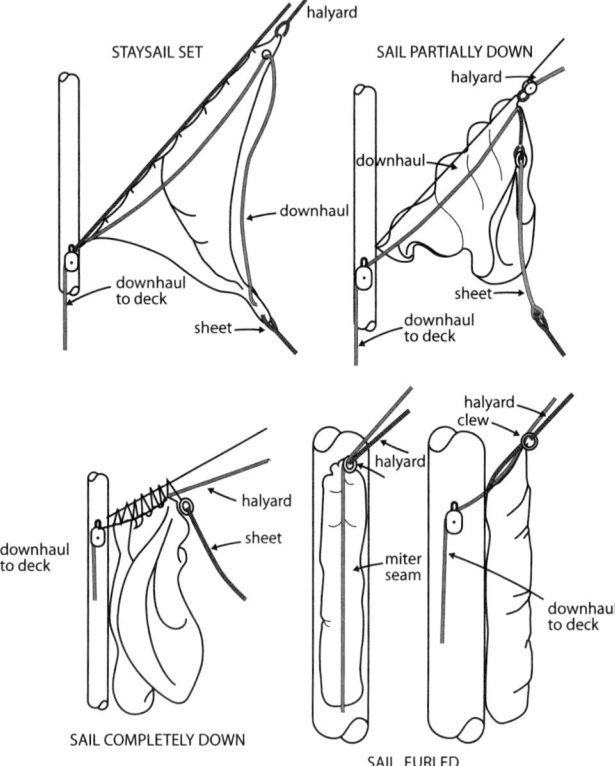

STAYSAIL SET

halyard

downhaul

downhaul to deck

sheet

SAIL PARTIALLY DOWN

halyard

downhaul

sheet

downhaul to deck

SAIL COMPLETELY DOWN

downhaul to deck

halyard

sheet

SAIL FURLED

halyard

miter seam

halyard
clew

downhaul to deck

forms a smooth cylinder. The bottom of the furl should be neatly squared off by tucking up any excess sailcloth. Gaskets should not be pulled so tightly as to disturb the tube shape of the furl.

Figure 17 illustrates the sequence of dousing a staysail and its appearance when doused. Headsails are harbor furled similarly and gaskets are secured to the bowsprit.

Harbor Furling Mizzensails

The lower and upper mizzensails are harbor furled exactly like a staysail except that there is no miter seam. A good furl resembles a tight cylinder. Since the foot of the sail is longer than the peak, there will be excess material at the foot. This material should be tucked in neatly so that only a tight skin can be seen.

The gaff topsail is an awkward sail to harbor furl. Like the other mizzensails, it is bulkier along the gaff. The sail should be tucked in so that a tight outer skin remains and so that as little sail as possible can be seen from on deck.

CHAPTER 7

Sailing Theory and Trim

Trimming sail to maximize ship speed is one of the greatest challenges for the officer of the deck, requiring constant attention and a true sense of the winds and seas and their combined effect on *Eagle*. The OOD and boatswain's mate of the watch (BMOW) work together closely to ensure that sails are properly trimmed and that the ship takes advantage of every wind shift.

Trimming sail requires a feel for the wind and sea, as well as an understanding of some basic principles. Square sails are trimmed with the braces, sheets, and course lifts; fore-and-aft sails are trimmed with their sheets. Before discussing trimming and sail balance, it is necessary to understand some of the basic forces involved.

The combination of forces acting on *Eagle* to propel her through the water is complex and difficult to analyze. For the purposes of trimming, however, only a few of these forces are discussed.

Aerodynamic force—Sails derive the bulk of their power from aerodynamic lift. A sail presents an aspect to the wind somewhat like that of an airplane wing, although a sail is uniformly thin as the wind passes from windward to leeward leech. The sail obtains driving power by altering the flow of the wind: trimmed properly, the weather leech and the first panel of sailcloth are in line with flow of the wind; as the sail curves aft toward the leeward leech, wind on the back of the sail compresses and creates high pressure, while the wind flow across the front of the sail diverges and creates low pressure (see fig. 18). In accordance with Bernoulli's principle, it is this pressure difference that pulls the sail forward. The direction of this resultant force can be divided into an athwartship component that causes heel and leeway, and a fore-and-aft component that draws the sail forward and drives the ship. The athwartship component is counteracted by the lateral resistance of the keel, which reduces leeway to a minimum.

Figure 18. Aerodynamic Lift

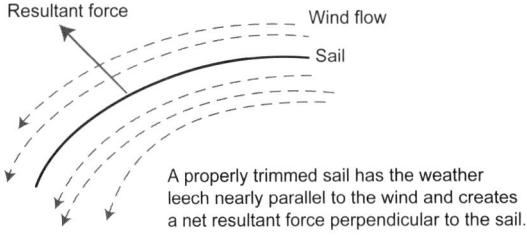

A properly trimmed sail has the weather leech nearly parallel to the wind and creates a net resultant force perpendicular to the sail.

As mentioned above, square sails are trimmed so that the weather leech and first panel of sailcloth are parallel to the wind so that there is a smooth airflow across both sides of the sail. Likewise, on fore-and-aft sails the luff should be at an angle parallel to the wind direction. When these angles are improper, turbulence and aerodynamic drag are created instead of lift, causing the sails to stall. Visually, if the wind is too far forward, the sail will *lift* or *luff* (see fig. 19).

Figure 19. Improper Trim

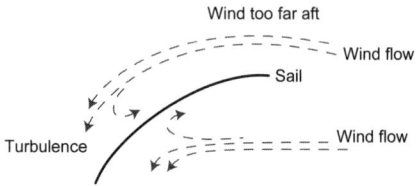

An improperly trimmed sail creates turbulence near the leeches, wasting valuable energy.

Figure 20. The Slot Effect

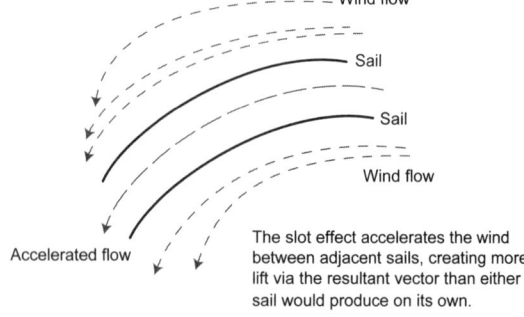

The slot effect accelerates the wind between adjacent sails, creating more lift via the resultant vector than either sail would produce on its own.

The slot effect—For fore-and-aft sails, there is a second important factor: the *slot* effect. The close proximity of the headsails and staysails to each other, when they are properly trimmed, forces the wind through the *slot* between the sails at a much higher velocity than if the sails were acting alone. This greater speed lowers the pressure on the leeward side of the windward sail, increasing lift and drive. Thus, staysails and especially headsails must be carefully trimmed relative to each other as well as to the wind (see fig. 20).

Impulse force—For aerodynamic lift to be effective, the wind direction must be virtually parallel to the windward leech of the sail (luff for fore-and-aft sails). Therefore, as *Eagle* bears off the wind (i.e., proceeding from close reach to beam reach to broad reach to run) aerodynamic lift is reduced until, when running downwind, there is no laminar (i.e., smooth) airflow across the sail; the sail does not act as an airfoil any longer. When the ship is running downwind, it is driven forward by the impulse force of the wind directly pushing on the sail area it encounters. At this point of sail, far less efficient than aerodynamic lift, driving force can only be increased by adding sail area; sails should be kept perpendicular to the wind to maximize this impulse force (see fig. 21).

Center of effort—Each sail has a center of effort; groups of sails, such as headsails or all fore square sails, have a center of effort; and there is a total center of effort for all sails set. The concept of center of effort is important to understand when dealing with sail balance.

Figure 21. Aerodynamic Lift vs. Impulse Force

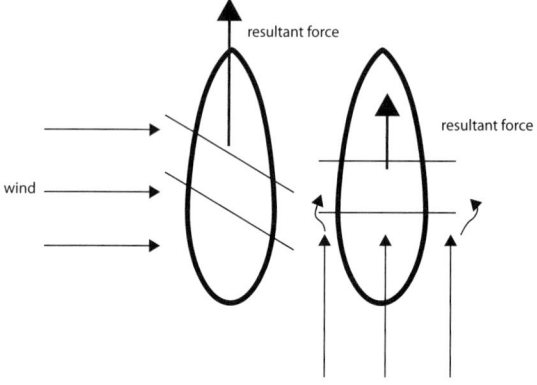

As the relative wind draws aft, the aerodynamic effects on the sails diminish until, when the wind is directly astern, only the impulse force remains, significantly less powerful than the aerodynamic effects when sailing on a reach.

Figure 22. Centers of Effort and Lateral Resistance

Combined center of effort for all sails when sailing full and by, with proper sail balance.
Note: slight weather helm necessary to maintain course.

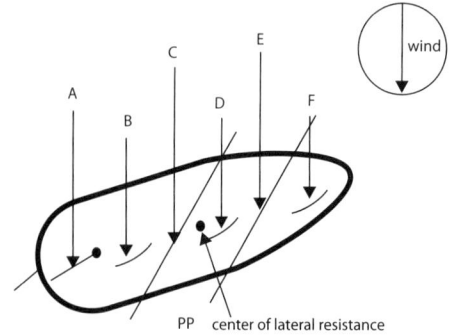

Center of lateral resistance—The center of lateral resistance is the center of the resistance to leeway created by the underwater body of the ship (see fig. 22). For smaller vessels, this is usually a centerboard or some type of keel. *Eagle* has a full-length finkeel. The center of lateral resistance changes with heel as the wetted surface area changes (i.e., as heel increases or fore-aft trim changes).

Trimming Fore and Aft Sails

Fore-and-aft sails derive the bulk of their power from aerodynamic lift. Hence, they are trimmed like the sails on a sloop or other fore-and-aft rigged vessels. Most of the power is created within the first few feet of the luff; it is particularly important that the halyard be hauled taut so that the luff has no scallops that would interfere with a smooth airflow. The sheet should be eased until the sail begins to lift and then sheeted back to the point where the lifting stops. All sails on a mast are trimmed to the wind and then to each other so that they do not backwind each other and ruin the slot effect.

The lower mizzen, upper mizzen, and gaff topsail are trimmed like the other fore-and-aft sails. They are joined along their leeches and therefore trimmed together. The aerodynamic effects of the large mizzensails are the same, but because of their distance from the pivot point, the mizzensails (particularly the lower mizzen) can produce a large turning moment and excessive weather helm if trimmed improperly. They can, however, produce tremendous driving power when trimmed properly. If excessive weather helm is observed, the OOD should first ensure that all sails forward are properly trimmed before easing the mizzen sheet or brailing in one or both of the mizzensails.

The headsails and the main staysails must also be trimmed in relationship to the square sails. Since yards can be braced only slightly more than 45 degrees from square to the ship, the square sails require *Eagle* to sail farther off the wind than a vessel with fore-and-aft sails alone. Hence, when square sails are set, the fore-and-aft sail sheets must be eased out farther than when sailing under fore-and-aft sails alone; if they are sheeted too flat, they will cause more leeway than driving power.

When on the wind the headsails and main staysails often backwind the leeward side of lower square sails. Although this may seem counterproductive, the driving power gained by the fore-and-aft sails can offset the loss of drive in the lower square sails. In short, the effect of each sail on all others must be considered. In setting, dousing, and trimming sails, the OOD must consider all of these effects to produce the best overall speed for the ship.

Fore-and-aft sails also produce driving force when the wind is from *astern* and aerodynamic force is no longer a factor. This force, however, is not nearly as significant since most of the sail area of the fore-and-aft sails is blanketed by the square sails when running downwind and since the fore-and-aft sails present relatively little sail area to the wind. The lower mizzen is the exception, since the mizzen boom can be used to haul the sail to port or starboard.

Trimming Square Sails

On a moving ship, the wind experienced on deck is not the *true wind* but rather the *relative wind*, which is a combination of the true wind and the ship's headway. On a ship that is moving ahead, the relative wind is always farther forward than the true wind. The faster the ship moves ahead, the farther forward the relative wind appears. Knowledge of relative wind is critical for any mariner (e.g., for flight operations, boat launch/recovery, etc.), but particularly so for those on a sailing ship (see fig. 23).

Figure 23. Relative Wind

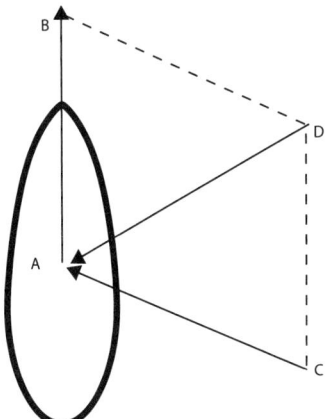

AB	Motion of the ship creates a relative wind directly opposite to the direction of the ship's motion and equal to its speed.
AC	True wind
AD	Resultant relative wind that strikes the sail. The faster the ship's forward motion AB, the farther forward will be the resultant relative wind AD.

Eagle's sails are always trimmed to the relative wind rather than the true wind. *Eagle* has numerous *telltales* (indicators of the relative wind): flags, pennants, and *anemometers* all assist the OOD and BMOW in trimming sail appropriately. It is important to note that the relative wind can be different on each mast, and especially at different heights in the rig.

Forces of aerodynamic lift are most effective when the relative wind is abeam or forward of the beam. When *Eagle* is *close-hauled*, the angle of attack of a square sail is very similar to that of a staysail. The leading edge of a square sail is the weather leech, analogous to the luff of a staysail. As previously mentioned, the weather leech should be trimmed to be nearly parallel to the relative wind. While an undertrimmed fore-and-aft sail will lift along its luff, a square sail lifts along the weather leech when the ship gets too close to the wind.

Practical Trimming

As previously discussed, both square and fore-and-aft sails are trimmed to ensure that the weather leech or luff, respectively, is parallel to the wind whenever the wind is abeam or forward of the beam. This ensures smooth airflow across the sails and maximizes aerodynamic lift. The diagram and table in figure 24 represent the angle of trim for the yards based on the angle of the relative wind. This table is just a starting point; the actual trim required for maximum speed depends on many factors, including wind velocity, heel of the ship, sea condition, and others. When fine-tuning the rig, yards are normally trimmed one *point* at a time, as shown in figure 24. When *braced sharp*, the yards form an angle of slightly more than 45 degrees, or four points, to the ship's head. At 90 degrees to the ship the yards are *braced square*. The intermediate points are named by their distance forward of being braced square. For instance, as the starboard yardarms move forward from being square, *Eagle* would be braced one point on a starboard tack, two points on a starboard tack, three points on a starboard tack, and finally braced sharp. Since there are fewer interferences high in the rig, it is

Figure 24. Bracing and Optimum Trim

A. Positions of the yards when trimming square sails

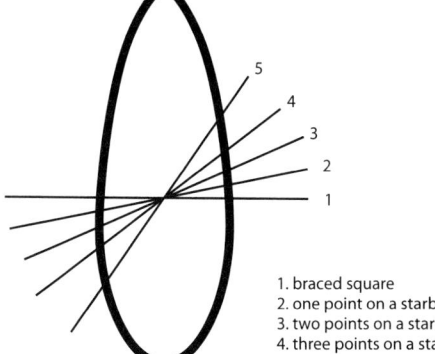

1. braced square
2. one point on a starboard tack
3. two points on a starboard tack
4. three points on a starboard tack
5. braced sharp (four points)

B. Theoretical optimum trim for square to maximize the combined aerodynamic lift and impulse force for different points of sail

Relative wind (degrees)	Best trim of yards	Angle of yards to relative wind
045 (broad on bow)	sharp (4 points)	0*
056 1/4 (3pts fwd of beam)	sharp	1 point
067 1/2 (2pts fwd of beam)	sharp (3 points)	1–2 points
078 3/4 (1pt fwd of beam)	3 points	2 points
090 (abeam)	2–3 points	2–3 points
101 1/4 (1pt aft the beam)	2 points	3 points
112 1/2 (2pts aft the beam)	1–2 points	3–4 points
123 3/4 (3pts aft the beam)	1 point	4 points
135 (broad on the quarter)	1 point (square)	4–5 points
146 1/4 (3pts on quarter)	square	5 points
157 1/2 (2pts on quarter)	square	6 points
168 3/4 (1pt on quarter)	square	7 points
180 (astern)	square	8 points

*squaresails will be lifting at 045 degees relative wind

possible to brace the upper yards farther than the lower yards. This is not done, however, because when braced sharp, yards are either *stacked* or *fanned*, as is described below.

As you can see in figure 24, *Eagle* cannot sail closer than about 75 degrees to the true wind. This point of sail is called close-hauled and is where *Eagle* sails most efficiently to windward. However, depending on the sea state and aloft winds, *Eagle* sails fastest somewhere between a close reach and a beam reach.

Assuming the true wind speed remains constant, as the wind draws abaft the beam the ship's speed generally decreases. Until the wind is abaft the beam, the yards should be trimmed to form an acute angle with the wind. This develops maximum driving power, allowing a smooth airflow across the sails, and minimizes turbulence. When the wind is abeam or forward of the beam, yards should be fanned to account for the change in angle of the relative wind striking the higher sails. The one exception to this rule is when trying to point *Eagle* as high into the wind as possible, albeit at the sacrifice of some speed; in this case of sailing *by the wind*, the yards should be stacked.

After the wind draws aft of the beam, aerodynamic lift forces decrease until they are minimal when running. At these points of sail, broad reach and running, the impulse force of the wind is driving the ship forward; therefore, yards are braced square to the wind. All other things being equal, running is the slowest point of sail because aerodynamic lift is no longer present and the main square sails *blanket* those on the fore. Also, the fore-and-aft sails will no longer fill properly when running downwind and must usually be doused. The mainsail may be *goosewinged* or even taken in during such circumstances to allow wind to pass through to the fore sails.

When running in light air, the sheets on the main square sails are sometimes soft-sheeted—by easing out two to five chain links on each sheet after all sails are set—to allow even more wind to pass through to the fore. As always, the yards should be stacked and cockbill removed. Sometimes when running downwind, it is advantageous to brace the fore yards square and brace the main yards to two or three points, attempting to keep the square sails on both masts filled and driving.

When at sea the yards should normally be braced sharp when the sails are not set. This is especially true when motoring into the wind, when there may be a difference of a knot or more in speed depending on whether the yards are braced to the wind or boxed against it. If the relative wind is 45 degrees or more aft of the bow, headsails and staysails can usually be carried, both reducing the rolling of the ship and providing additional speed.

Yard Fanning

As one moves higher above the surface of the ocean, the true wind is subject to less friction; therefore, wind speed increases with altitude. In other words, the wind is fairer aloft. On a ship moving ahead, this means the relative wind moves aft with increased height. *Fanning* the yards allows *Eagle*'s OOD to take advantage of this differential velocity by exposing more sail area optimally to the wind aloft. In fanning, the weather yardarms are progressively braced farther aft on each higher yard, allowing each sail to present the optimal angle of attack to the relative wind.

Sometimes the topgallants and royals are fanned back even more than is optimal to act as a telltale to the OOD. When braced back, they will begin to lift (or even luff) before the lower sails and thus serve as a warning to trim sail or fall off before the ship is caught aback. When braced sharp in light air, the yards are fanned properly when each yard on the weather side can be seen just aft of the one below it when viewed from under the course yard.

Sail Balance

As *Eagle* moves through the water, numerous forces act upon her hull, superstructure, and rigging. These forces can sometimes be difficult to understand. To explain the basic concepts, we will call a certain point on the ship the pivot point. The location of this pivot point depends on several factors, including the ship's speed, trim, and wetted surface area, but when making headway it is usually found amidships in the vicinity of the galley. If the forces acting forward of this point are in equilibrium with those acting aft of it, the ship will move forward in a straight line with no weather helm.

If the sails are not in balance, either weather or lee helm will be present. Weather helm occurs when, with the rudder amidships, the ship tends to round up into the wind; *lee helm* occurs when the ship tends to fall off. Referring back to figure 22, you can see that the headsails and foresails are forward of the pivot point (PP), the main staysails are close to the pivot point, while the remaining sails and the rudder are aft of the point. If the sails set are not carefully balanced, there will be a greater force either forward or aft of the pivot point. When the center of effort of all the sails set is directly above the center of lateral resistance, the ship will be in balance.

Eagle, like most sailing vessels, is designed to sail with slight weather helm. This ensures that the ship will luff up into the wind and lose way in the event of a steering casualty or other emergency. Slight weather helm also gives the OOD a better feel of the ship, allowing course changes to be made to compensate for wind shifts without relying solely on the compass or telltales. Properly balanced, *Eagle* usually carries about 7 degrees of weather helm when sailing close-hauled. More weather helm can sometimes be carried without losing speed, particularly in a good breeze.

Eagle's rudder is comparably larger than the rudder on most power-driven vessels. In addition to turning the ship, however, it can act as a brake whose effect (because of the resistance of the water) can offset the driving power of several sails. It is beneficial to carry as little rudder angle as possible while still keeping as many sails set as possible.

As winds increase, *Eagle* will increasingly heel to leeward. Heeling actually slows the vessel and can be dangerous if it becomes excessive. Excessive heel also causes the airflow across the sails to be disturbed, resulting in less driving power. Additionally, the bow will dig in and the keel will present less lateral resistance, resulting in more leeway. Some heeling is acceptable, but the OOD must always be cognizant of the "feel" of the ship and be prepared to douse upper sails or cautiously fall off to reduce heel (care must be taken when falling off to ensure that *Eagle* is not caught by the lee by having the stern inadvertently pass through the wind).

Decisions as to the order and number of sails to be set should be made keeping sail balance in mind. Each sail must be properly trimmed to ensure that the overall sail balance can be achieved. The lower and upper mizzensails are particularly important in sail balance. As large sails well aft of the pivot point, they create a large turning moment. As a result, the mizzen boom must sometimes be eased out beyond the mizzensails' optimum point of sail to eliminate excessive weather helm. This generally occurs in light air. When the wind is on the *quarter*, it may even be necessary to brail in one or both mizzensails; the speed lost by brailing in is compensated for by the decreased rudder drag.

When excessive weather helm is observed, however, the OOD should not immediately ease the mizzen boom or brail in the mizzensails. Many times the problem is found in improperly trimmed sails forward of the pivot point (e.g., fore yards not braced sharp or not fanned, headsails sheeted in too far, or excessive cockbill).

Cockbill

As the ship heels in a wind, the yards will *cockbill* with respect to the horizon. As a result the wind, which essentially travels parallel to the water's surface, will not strike the sails parallel to the sail heads and flow smoothly off to leeward. Instead it will flow at an angle up and over the yards, causing an excessive amount of turbulence and a drop in efficiency and speed. Thus, the yards must be trimmed parallel to the horizon using the course lifts.

When the square sails are set, the cockbill of all sails can be adjusted at once by using the course lifts; they are effectively connected to the remaining yards through the leeches of the sails. In adjusting course lifts, the lee course sheet and tack must be eased as the yard moves up while the weather sheet and tack are rounded in. The leeward braces on the lower three yards will also have to be eased since they will bind as the lee lift is hauled.

The yards are kept cockbilled at the same angle when braced sharp with the sails furled, in order to present a neater appearance and to prevent the lower topsail yard from being fouled as the upper topsail yard cockbills. If the course yards are allowed to cockbill, the tack and sheet on the side on which the yard is moving forward (weather side) will grow taut as the yard cockbills upward and must be eased while the opposite tack and sheet must be rounded in. If the yards are not parallel after bracing, the lower topsail yard, which does not have a

Figure 25. Cockbill

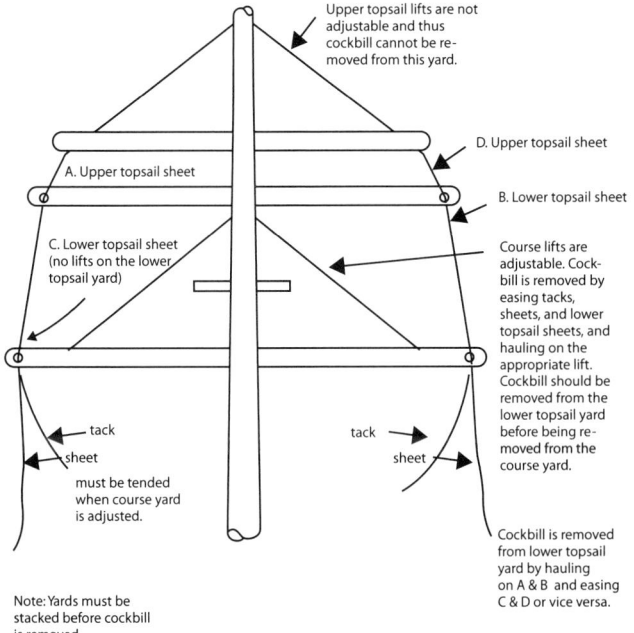

Procedures for removing cockbill. Sails are not set.

Upper topsail lifts are not adjustable and thus cockbill cannot be removed from this yard.

D. Upper topsail sheet

A. Upper topsail sheet

B. Lower topsail sheet

C. Lower topsail sheet (no lifts on the lower topsail yard)

Course lifts are adjustable. Cockbill is removed by easing tacks, sheets, and lower topsail sheets, and hauling on the appropriate lift. Cockbill should be removed from the lower topsail yard before being removed from the course yard.

tack

tack

sheet

sheet

must be tended when course yard is adjusted.

Cockbill is removed from lower topsail yard by hauling on A & B and easing C & D or vice versa.

Note: Yards must be stacked before cockbill is removed.

lift, can most easily be paralleled to the upper topsail yard by adjusting the sheets of the lower and upper topsails. In figure 25, the four sheets form two opposing pairs. The course yards can be adjusted by throwing off the lower topsail sheets and adjusting the lifts.

Bracing (with Sails Furled)

Because of the numerous other lines that are affected when the yards are moved, bracing is more complicated than merely hauling on the braces on one side and easing them on the other. In general, the buntlines, leechlines, bunt-leechlines, and (to a lesser extent) the sheets and clewlines will become taut on the side of the yard that is to be braced forward (new weather side) and will become slack on the side that is to be braced aft (new lee side). Collectively these lines on the new weather side are called the lee gear. If they are not properly handled, lines may part, bull's eyes and lizards may be pulled out, or the sail may rip.

Due to the their fixed lifts, when sails are not set, bracing always results in the upper three yards becoming cockbilled as they are more sharply braced. The cause of cockbill when sails are not set can be seen by examining the case of the fixed lifts in figure 26. The lifts lead from fittings on the sides of the mast to the yardarms (see fig. 26c). When a yard is braced (to port in this case), it pivots on a pin on the yard shoe (O). Yards theoretically swing in the horizontal arc (A-A' and B-B'). The fixed lifts, however, pivot at their fittings on the sides of the mast (at C and E) and can swing only in an arc (D-D' and F-F'). Since the lifts of the upper three yards are not adjustable, the yard cannot actually swing in a horizontal arc from A to A'. It is canted upward, or cockbilled, as the port lift becomes taut (as shown in fig. 26b). The opposite yardarm cockbills downward and takes

Figure 26. Cockbill as a Result of Bracing

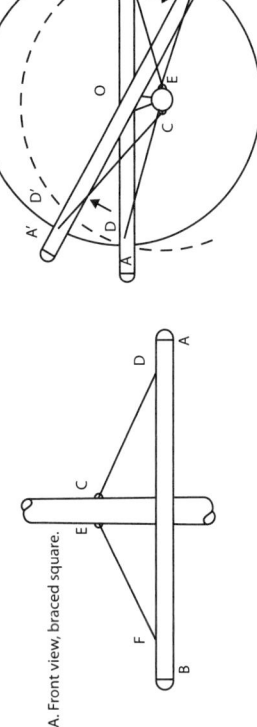

A. Front view, braced square.

B. Front view, braced on port tack. Since lifts are not adjustable on the upper three yards, the yard cockbills upward on the side moving forward.

yardarm moving forward cants upward.

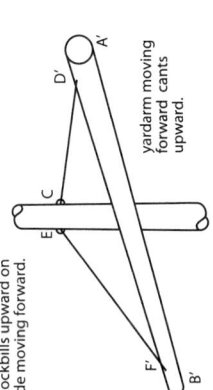

C. Top view, bracing toward port tack. The yard pivots at O forward of the mast but the lifts pivot at C and E on the side of the mast. Since lifts, except on the courses, are not adjustable, the yardarm must rise on the side that is braced forward (here the port) and drop on the side that moves aft. One lift (CD) comes taut and cants the yard upward and the other lift (EF) becomes slack and allows the yard to cant downward.

up the slack gained in the starboard lift. This principle is most easily understood by climbing aloft and actually examining the yards when they are in their fixed lifts.

The lifts on the courses are adjustable. It is possible, therefore, to brace these yards without developing cockbill by easing the lift on the side on which the yard is being braced forward (new weather side) and by hauling on the opposite lift (on the same side as the braces that are being hauled). The lower topsail yard has no lifts and will parallel the upper topsail yard if the upper topsail sheets are belayed. Since the lower topsail leeches link the lower topyard and course yard when the lower topsail is set, the upper topsail sheets may have to be eased when bracing around if the upper topsail is furled. And, as mentioned previously, the course lifts will take the cockbill out of all upper yards whose square sail is set.

Just as the lifts are affected by bracing, so too are the buntlines, bunt-leechlines, and leechlines, whose leads are approximately the same as the lifts. As the yardarm moves forward, the lines become taut and may part, pull out lizards or bull's eyes, or tear the sail—especially when the sails are harbor furled. On the opposite side, the lines will slacken. Thus, in bracing, the lines on the side on which the yardarm is moving forward must be taken off their pin or, at least, eased and belayed. Clewlines and sheets lead along the edge of the yard and pivot fairly close to where the yard itself pivots. As a result, they are less affected by the movement of the yard. Nevertheless, if they are snug before the bracing evolution begins, they will become taut and possibly part on the side on which the yard is moving forward.

On the main, the proximity of the braces to the boat davits often causes problems. Unless handled carefully, the main braces can foul on the after davit. The timenoguy is a *whip* running from the mizzen shrouds to the main brace and is used to haul the brace clear of the davits. It may be necessary to station a person with a special U-shaped boat hook near the davit to keep the brace clear.

The commands and procedures for bracing occur in the following sequence.

1. Preparatory steps include faking out the appropriate braces, tacks, and sheets for running. All clewlines, buntlines, buntleechlines, and leechlines (lee gear) on the side on which the yardarm is to move forward (new weather side) should be taken off their pins. To adjust cockbill while bracing, the course lifts should be manned and taken off the pins.

2. Bracing around:
    a. Mast captain: *"On the main braces. Ease port. Haul around starboard. Tend your tacks and sheets."*
    b. Because of the differences in the purchases of the braces and the weights of the yards, the royal and topgallant yards will normally come around faster than the lower three yards. The mast captain usually delegates the responsibility of keeping the yards moving together to the brace captain. The mast captain may give the order *"Handsomely," "Lively,"* or *"That's well on the main royal (topgallant, etc.) brace,"* if the yards are not being braced together.
    c. If bracing square or bracing sharp, those easing the braces should ease them out until they reach their *leather.* The leathers consist of short strips of leather that are tucked into the strands of the lines after the braces have been stretched out to mark the proper position for the yard when it is square or braced sharp with a fan.

d. Once the yards are in position, all slack must be taken out of the braces. This must be done before sending personnel out on the yards or before securing the evolution, to keep the yards from moving and possibly damaging gear or causing someone to lose footing.

Bracing (with Sails Set)

Bracing the yards with the sails set is similar to bracing with the sails furled. With the upper three yards up, however, the fixed lifts hang slack. All of the yards are now joined through the leeches of their sails. Thus, it is possible to remove the cockbill from all five yards by adjusting the course lifts. The yards should be kept parallel to the horizon to allow the best angle for smooth flow of wind over the sails. When bracing with all sail set, the inertia of the tremendous weight of the gear will often result in the yards cockbilling, even if the course lifts are off their pins. For this reason, it is necessary to haul on the fore and main lifts on the side on which the braces are being hauled so that the yards can be kept parallel to the horizon. While the yards are in motion, three or four people can adjust the lifts; once the yards are braced, many more will be needed to do the same job, and tacks, sheets, and other braces will have to be handled. The lift that is hauled to remove cockbill is always the lee lift once the yards have been braced.

The wind usually strikes the sail at such an angle that the weather braces have more strain than the lee braces, so more people will be needed to brace when the sails are set than when they are doused. If the courses remain set, it is particularly important to have sufficient people on the sheet that will be hauled. It is also important that the personnel assigned to the eased tack and sheet pay particular attention not to let the lines run away, which could cause severe rope burns.

Similarly, those easing the braces must not lose control and let the yards slam up against the backstays. Not only is this dangerous, but it is a tremendous waste of manpower and time. One person easing the weather brace too far will require the work of many people to haul the yard against the wind to its correct position. There is no excuse for yards being braced too far, especially with leathers properly adjusted.

Before bracing from the sharp position, the tack jigger must be cleared away. Again, the lee gear must be removed from the pins on the side on which the yardarm will move forward. Sheets, which remain belayed, should be watched carefully in case they become too taut and jam in the cheek block on the yardarm, although sheets are normally not a problem with sails set.

The commands for bracing with the sails set are the same as those given when the sails are doused, except that the command *"Haul around on the port (starboard) lift"* will be given as appropriate.

CHAPTER 8

Introduction to Working the Ship

O ver the centuries square-rigger sailors have developed an intimacy with the sea that modern-day seamen find hard to emulate. Those who dedicated their lives to sailing such vessels relied solely on the wind and sea for the success or failure of their voyage. Today *Eagle* requires the same dedication and skill from those who sail her that is now part of square-rigger folklore. As in days gone by, *Eagle* must use the wind to its best advantage; the next chapters focus on how to best accomplish this.

Under full sail *Eagle* can point to within about 75 degrees of the true wind. In certain conditions she can point to within about 55 degrees of the true wind; despite her sails filling, her leeway becomes increasingly dramatic. Her fore-and-aft sails alone will carry as close as about 45 degrees off the relative wind. In practice, however, *Eagle* is sailed under fore-and-aft sails alone only when motorsailing; this is done to gain added speed and decrease rolling.

Whenever a sailing vessel's destination lies farther upwind than she can sail, it is necessary to slowly work up to windward by zigzagging back and forth in a series of tacks. Without deviating too far from her intended trackline, the vessel gains as much distance upwind as possible on each leg. Then she will come about or tack by putting the wind on the other side, and continue to work upwind until the final destination is reached.

For a square-rigger this is a very long and arduous process. Gaining a short distance to windward will require sailing many miles overall and tacking numerous times. A square-rigger does not sail well upwind and may actually lose ground if not properly handled. Therefore, proper sail trim and taking advantage of every wind shift is essential when sailing close-hauled. Equally important is the ability to tack or wear quickly with a minimum loss of ground.

There are three basic methods of changing tacks: *tacking*, where the bow is brought through the wind; *wearing*, where the stern is brought through; and *boxhauling*, where elements of a tack and a wear are combined to allow the ship to come about in a minimum amount of sea room. Of these three, tacking is the preferred method. Tacking takes less time, loses less ground, and only requires the bow to swing through about 150 degrees. On the other hand, wearing is a relatively slow evolution, requires turning through about 210 degrees, and carries the ship downwind throughout the entire evolution, thereby losing valuable ground gained to windward.

When wearing, the staysails are doused and the mizzensails are brailed in before the evolution begins. Also, the foresails are blanketed by the main square sails for much of the evolution. As a result, wearing takes much longer, usually twenty minutes or more. Wearing is relatively easy to understand, however, and can be safely executed in almost any weather.

Tacking is more difficult, and teamwork and timing are critical. A tack can be accomplished in less than half the time of a wear—five to six minutes with a trained crew. If preparation time is included, the advantage of tacking is even more apparent. Most important, however, is that the ship can actually gain distance upwind while tacking, since the turn is made into the wind and not downwind. Since all sails remain set while preparing for the evolution, even more ground is gained and ship speed is maintained longer than when wearing.

There are situations, however, where the ship cannot or should not tack. In tacking, the fore square sails are brought aback, where they act as a huge brake. In light winds the ship may not have enough way to overcome this braking effect. In higher winds it may be dangerous to put the square sails aback. This danger becomes quite evident if you recall *Eagle*'s mast support as described in chapter 3. The masts are supported primarily by shrouds and backstays that oppose the wind force on the after side of the sails. They are also supported by stays that lead forward from the masts. However, there are far fewer forward-leading stays than back backstays and shrouds.

In general *Eagle* should not be tacked when the true wind speed exceeds about 25 knots, because of the danger to the rig (making over 12 knots through the water). Also, *Eagle* will usually not tack in winds of less than 10 knots, because she will not have enough speed to make it through the wind (when making less than 5 knots through the water). These speeds provide only a rough rule of thumb. In flat-calm seas the ship may tack when sailing in winds of less than 10 knots, and in heavier seas she may miss stays in winds of 15 knots or more.

Finally, tacking is an evolution that requires all hands on deck. If only a small number of personnel are available, as in a normal watch section, it is only practical to wear rather than tack.

Boxhauling is used when it is necessary to come about in a minimum of space, as in a crowded harbor or confined channel.

It combines the elements of a tack and a wear. The ship first turns upwind, is caught aback, then falls off onto the original tack and finally wears around onto the new tack. Boxhauling may also be used to recover from an unsuccessful tack, where the ship has come dead in the water before coming through the wind.

CHAPTER 9

Working the Ship: Tacking

A successful tack requires careful preparation, teamwork, and execution, as well as an understanding of the forces affecting the ship. When *Eagle* tacks, all hands are on deck and trainees face one of their greatest challenges at sea. All hands must be organized to establish a clear chain of command; they must not only memorize the commands but also develop an understanding of the forces and basic principles involved. The OOD will give the commands and is in control of the evolution. A forehanded OOD will develop a thorough understanding of this chapter before assuming the watch. The three mast captains will carry out the orders of the OOD at their respective masts.

For a successful tack, a square-rigger must be sailing *full and by*. The ship should be sailed as close to the wind as possible, to minimize the distance she has to turn through the wind. On the other hand, the vessel must be sailed off the wind far enough that the best possible speed is maintained to ensure that the bow will pass through the wind.

Additionally, the sails should be handled to help rather than hinder the swing of the ship. The headsails and mizzensails are the farthest from the pivot point; in addition to driving the ship forward they also impart a turning moment about the pivot point that can be used to help bring the ship through the wind. These will be important sails to handle during the tack.

Eagle, like most sailing vessels, carries slight weather helm whenever she is sailing close-hauled. Therefore, with all sails set, the ship naturally wants to turn into the wind. This natural force should be taken advantage of when coming about. The amount of rudder used during a tacking evolution is highly dependent on the weather conditions at the time. Often, applying full rudder will quickly swing the bow to windward, assisting the tack. There are also occasions where applying only a moderate amount of rudder will be sufficient to tack and will help keep speed on the ship, crucial during light-air evolutions.

By far, the most important element in the tack is for the OOD to ensure that *Eagle* is sailing full and by and that all sails are properly trimmed before the evolution begins. *Pinching*, or sailing *off the wind*, is frequently the cause of missing *stays*. Regardless of how the sails are handled or the timing of the commands, if *Eagle* is not sailing close to the wind with all sails drawing properly, she may not have enough momentum to make it through the wind.

Mast captains are responsible for trimming sails on their mast before reporting *"Manned and ready."* For the square sails, yards are usually fanned, cockbill removed, weather leeches taut, and all gear overhauled. All sheets on the fore-and aft sails are properly trimmed and scallops are removed along the luffs.

Before tacking, all necessary gear must be carefully faked out. A jammed brace, for example, can cause the ship to miss stays. A jammed halyard may result in a torn sail. To prevent such a mishap, staysail halyards and sheets, as well as the lee braces, must be faked out for running. Buntlines, bunt-leechlines, leechlines, and clewlines must be taken off their pins on the lee side to prevent them from coming taut and parting as the yards are braced. The tack jiggers are usually cleared away while readying the gear. The foresail, however, provides significant driving power and balances the turning force of the mizzensails. Thus, in marginal tacking conditions, the tack jigger should remain boarded until just before the command *"Let go and haul."*

When all masts report *"Manned and ready,"* the informational command *"Helm's alee" is* given. The mizzen boom is hauled amidships and the rudder command is given to start the turn upwind. Hauling the mizzen boom amidships helps force the stern downwind and allows the mizzensails to continue to draw as the bow turns up into the wind.

If trimmed properly, the headsails will luff as soon as the ship starts the turn upwind. They should be watched closely to ensure that they do not slat about, but they should not be sheeted flat, which would hinder the swing of the ship. The remaining sails are kept drawing to drive the ship forward. Sometimes the mizzen staysails are sheeted slightly flatter than normal to allow them to carry longer, to keep them driving forward and to help swing the stern downwind.

As the ship turns into the wind, the square sails will eventually start to lift (and then luff) and will become ineffective. At this point the mainsail is brought up into its gear. This is done for three reasons. First, if left set the mainsail would quickly *back* and would act as a huge brake, since it is the largest sail. In addition, the leads of the mainsail sheets and tacks are extremely long, so it is very difficult to handle them when bracing; the associated linehandlers can be used more effectively elsewhere. Finally, by bringing the mainsail up into its gear, the OOD has a clear view forward and can more easily control the evolution. With an untrained or reduced crew, the mainsail is sometimes brought up into its gear before the evolution begins to ensure that there are enough hands to execute the command *"Mainsail haul."*

While the mainsail is being hauled up into its gear, the main staysails are also being doused. These sails may still be filling but not to their best advantage, and since they will soon be luffing, they can easily be spared. It is easier to douse them when they are slightly filled than when they are luffing violently. This enables a small number of trainees to shift their sheets to the new tack and to have them ready to reset by the time the ship is through the wind, reducing the overall time for completion of the maneuver. Most important, these staysail handlers will be available within a short time to be hauling on the braces. The mizzen staysails, on the other hand, are held as long as they will fill. This provides additional drive as well as a force aft of the pivot point.

As the ship continues to turn, the upper square sails on the main will begin to back. The command *"Mainsail haul"* is then given, and the main yards are hauled around to the new tack. This action—the most critical of the entire evolution—requires precise timing. If not timed correctly, the ship may not make it through the wind. If the yards are hauled around too soon, much of the main sail area, which would otherwise be blanketed by the fore, will be fully exposed to the wind and act as a brake (see fig. 27). If the yards are hauled around too late, the main square sails will back along their entire width and a tremendous amount of manpower will be needed to haul the braces. This causes the yards to be braced more slowly, resulting in decreased speed or in *Eagle* gaining sternway.

The proper time for the command is when the weather half of the main square sails are aback. Bracing at this time allows the wind to do most of the work, since most of the mainmast

Figure 27. Tacking: Timing for Mainsail Haul

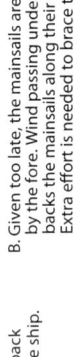

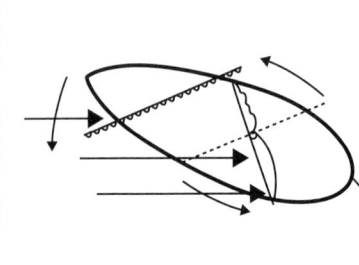
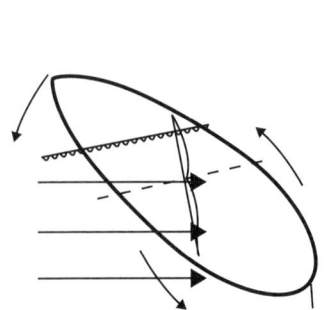

A. Given too soon, the mainsails back and act as a brake, stopping the ship.

B. Given too late, the mainsails are blanketed by the fore. Wind passing under the foresails backs the mainsails along their entire width. Extra effort is needed to brace the yards.

C. Given at the proper time, the wind backs only the weather edge of the mainsails and forces the yards around. Only the wind passing under the foresails strikes the lee side of the mainsails.

sail area is blanketed by the fore. If timed correctly only a minimum amount of effort is needed once the yards begin moving onto their new tack. The lee braces are eased rapidly out to their leathers while the weather braces are hauled. The yards must be kept under control and must not run past their leathers, to prevent them from slamming up against the backstays and causing damage. As the yards move, there may be slack in the lee braces and sometimes even in the weather braces. One person should be stationed on each mizzen pinrail to man the timenoguy to prevent the main braces from fouling on the boat davits.

As the bow comes through the wind, the headsail sheets are shifted onto the new tack. If the ship has come dead in the water before the bow comes through the wind, however, the headsail sheet should be backed on the original tack to increase their turning effect. The mizzen boom is eased so that it does not force the stern downwind, and the rudder is put amidships.

As the ship continues to swing onto the new tack and the mainsails begin to draw, the command *"Let go and haul"* is given; the fore yards are then braced onto the new tack. As soon as possible thereafter, the main and the mizzen staysails are reset, followed by the mainsail. Unless otherwise ordered, all sails set on the old tack are reset on the new; if the course tacks were boarded on the old tack, they will be boarded on the new. All sails are trimmed to their best advantage without further order.

At times the ship will come dead in the water while she is head to wind. *Eagle* will then gain sternway very rapidly and the rudder must be shifted to allow the bow to fall off onto the new tack. With the fore square sails aback, the ship can usually gain enough sternway to *back* around onto the new tack.

Occasionally the ship will not properly answer her helm in such conditions. She is then said to be *in irons*.

When caught in irons it is usually beneficial to brail in the mizzensails, to eliminate their tendency to keep the bow into the wind. If the bow fails to pass through the wind and the ship falls off onto the original tack, *Eagle* is said to have missed stays; the main yards must be rebraced, the staysails reset, and speed built up again to attempt another tack. If time is of the essence, it may be better to consider the unsuccessful tack as the first part of a boxhaul (see chapter 10).

Organization and teamwork are critically important in tacking. Throughout the Age of Sail, crews of twenty or less routinely tacked vessels much larger than *Eagle*. The large complement of personnel on board *Eagle* allows a tack to be accomplished more expeditiously and with less individual effort. It requires closer supervision, however, because of the relative inexperience of the trainees and because a single brace or halyard improperly faked out or untended may cause the ship to miss stays.

The foremast personnel should initially man the main staysail downhauls and prepare for bracing. The foremast personnel are free during the first half of a tack and handle the main staysail downhauls, as the mainmast personnel will be busy handling the staysails and mainsail and laying aft to haul the main braces. As soon as the main staysails are doused, the personnel on the fore can lay to their braces, foresail tacks, and sheets, then stand by to brace the fore yards.

As previously mentioned, the tack jigger must be cleared away on the courses before bracing can begin. Since the foresail is a large driving sail, however, the tack jigger should not be cleared away too early or the loss of driving power may result in missing stays. The foresail is also important in sail balance and offsets the force aft of the mizzensails. If the tack jigger is cleared away too early, excess weather helm may slow the ship in addition to the loss of driving power.

Mainmast personnel should man the mainsail gear, the staysail halyards, and the sheets for the main staysails. Personnel assigned to the mainsail tacks and sheets should remain at their stations because the yards will be braced almost immediately after the mainsail has been taken in. As mentioned earlier, if the yards are hauled at the right time the wind will do much of the work.

After the mainsail has been taken in, personnel assigned to the staysails and clew-garnets should lay aft to the braces to assist in hauling the mainsail. In a good breeze the command *"Mainsail haul"* is given almost immediately following *"Rise tacks and sheets."* Thus, careful stationing of personnel is essential if mainmast personnel are to be ready to respond to both commands when directed. The mainsail is not reset until the staysails have been reset, all yards have been properly fanned or stacked, and cockbill taken out for the new tack.

Mizzen personnel should man the mizzen staysail gear, the mizzen sheet, vangs, preventer, and flag halyards. The mizzen boom is hauled against the wind, so as many trainees as possible should be stationed on the mizzen sheet. Hauling in the mizzen boom also requires personnel to ease the preventer and tend the vangs and flag halyards. Once this is accomplished these personnel should assist with the mizzen staysail downhauls.

Normally a single person is assigned to each of the staysail halyards, two to each sheet, and one to each of the mainsail tacks and sheets. An upperclass supervisor and two or three trainees should be assigned to shift the staysail sheets once the staysails have been doused. Working steadily, they can have all of the sails ready to be reset by the time the bow has passed through the wind. One trainee is stationed in the tops before the evolution begins to stand by to shift the staysail sheet pendants.

Tacking: Step by Step

The commands and procedures for tacking occur in a particular sequence (given below). The commands for tacking are shown in figure 28.

1. Preparatory steps:
    a. OOD: *"All hands to sail stations."*
    b. Mast captains: *"Fore (main, mizzen) manned"* (when enough personnel are at the mast to handle sail).
    c. OOD: *"Ready about."* This command means prepare to tack.
    d. Mast captains: *"Fore (main, mizzen) manned and ready."* This report should not be given until all lines that will run have been faked out; all lee clewlines, buntlines, bunt-leechlines, and leechlines have been taken off their pins; all lines are manned; and everyone is ready to start the evolution.

2. Bringing ship into the wind:
    a. OOD: *"Helm's alee."* This is an informational command notifying all personnel that the maneuver has begun.
    b. OOD to mizzenmast captain: *"Haul the mizzen boom amidships."*
    c. OOD to helmsman: *"Right (Left) full rudder."* The rudder command is normally given as the mizzen boom begins moving amidships. If the command is timed correctly, the mizzensails will continue to drive the ship

Figure 28. Tacking

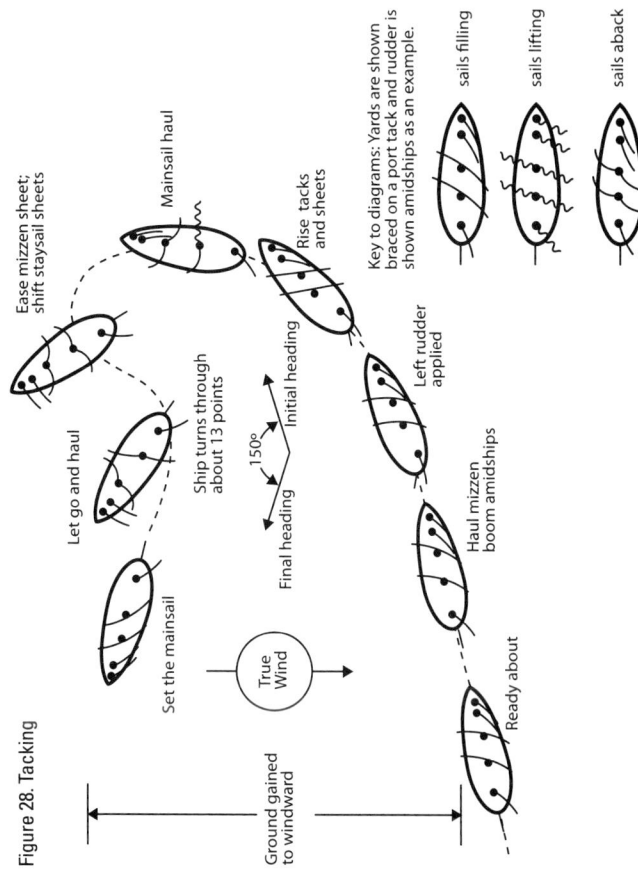

Ease mizzen sheet;
shift staysail sheets

Mainsail haul

Let go and haul

Set the mainsail

Ship turns through
about 13 points

Initial heading

150°

Final heading

Rise tacks
and sheets

Left rudder
applied

Key to diagrams: Yards are shown
braced on a port tack and rudder is
shown amidships as an example.

sails filling

sails lifting

sails aback

Haul mizzen
boom amidships

Ready about

True
Wind

Ground gained
to windward

forward as the turn upwind is made, and they will also provide a turning moment.

3.   Bracing the main:
   a.   OOD to main and mizzenmast captains: *"Rise tacks and sheets."* This command is given when the weather leeches of the main square sails begin to lift. On this command the mainmast captain takes in the mainsail and douses the main staysails, and the mizzenmast captain douses the mizzen staysails. There is no separate command from the OOD concerning the staysails. As discussed earlier, the mizzenmast captain usually holds the mizzen staysails as long as possible to take advantage of their driving power and turning effect. However, the mizzen staysails must be kept under control at all times to keep from endangering bridge personnel.
   b.   OOD to mainmast captain: *"Mainsail haul."* This command should be given as soon as the weather leeches of the main square sails begin to back.

4.   Head to the wind:
   a.   OOD to foremast captain: *"Shift the headsail sheets,"* or, if the vessel has lost headway and risks not coming through the wind, *"Lead aft the lee sheets,"* in which case the headsails are reset flat on the old tack so that they will back and help swing the bow off onto the new tack.
   b.   OOD to mizzenmast captain: *"Ease the mizzen boom."* The mizzen boom is eased out as far as necessary so that it will not hold the bow up into the wind.
   c.   The OOD should give orders to the helm as appropriate. If the ship's head comes through the wind, the rudder should be eased to prevent the vessel from swinging

too far off the wind on the new tack and losing ground downwind. If the ship comes dead in the water and then gains sternway, the rudder should be shifted to back the ship around onto the new tack.

5. Once on the new tack:

   a. OOD to foremast captain: *"Let go and haul."* This command is given when the mainsails begin to fill. The fore yards are braced around quickly to the new tack. Note: if the command *"Mainsail haul"* is slow to be executed, the command *"Let go and haul"* should be given as soon as the bow has passed well through the wind. Waiting for the main to be braced in this case simply results in added leeway and more time until the ship regains headway.

   b. OOD to main and mizzenmast captains: *"Set the mainsail."* On this command, first the main and mizzen staysails are reset, followed by the mainsail. No further commands are needed from the OOD.

   c. After all sails are set, each mast captain trims sail and fans the yards appropriately for the new tack. When braced sharp, the fore and main yards should be fanned unless the OOD directs otherwise.

CHAPTER 10

Working the Ship:
Wearing and Boxhauling

As described in chapter 8, there are three basic methods of changing tacks: tacking, where the bow is brought through the wind; wearing, where the stern is brought through; and boxhauling, where elements of a tack and a wear are combined to allow the ship to come about in a minimum amount of sea room.

When wearing, the staysails are doused and the mizzensails are brailed in before the evolution begins. Also, the foresails are blanketed by the main square sails for much of the evolution. As a result, wearing takes much longer than tacking, usually twenty minutes or more. Wearing is relatively easy to understand, however, and can be safely executed in almost any weather, even with only the watch on deck if necessary.

Boxhauling is used when it is necessary to come about in a minimum of space, as in a crowded harbor or confined channel. It combines the elements of a tack and a wear. The ship first turns upwind, is caught aback, then falls off onto the original tack and finally wears around onto the new tack. Boxhauling may also be used to recover from an unsuccessful tack, where the ship has come dead in the water before coming through the wind.

Wearing

Wearing with a Full Crew (Simultaneous Wearing)

The organization and preparation necessary for wearing is noticeably less than for a tack. The mizzensails are brailed in and the staysails are all doused before beginning the wear. As in tacking, the lee buntlines, bunt-leechlines, leechlines, and clewlines should be taken off their pins. All gear that is to run should be carefully faked out.

A few personnel should be assigned to shift the sheets on the main and mizzen staysails, while the remainder can man the braces. A single person is required for each mainsail tack and sheet unless the wind is strong. Four or five people will be needed for each new lee lift. The number of personnel needed for the foresail sheets varies with the wind conditions but normally does not exceed four or five for each sheet. During the entire evolution, mizzen personnel are engaged in hauling the mizzen boom to the new tack, rigging the preventer, shifting the sheets for the mizzen staysails, and assisting with bracing the main yards.

The commands and procedures for simultaneous wearing occur in a particular sequence (given below). The commands for simultaneous wearing are shown in figure 29.

1. Preparatory stage:
   a. OOD: *"All hands to sail stations."*
   b. Mast captains: *"Fore (main, mizzen) manned"* (when enough personnel are at the mast to handle sail).
   c. OOD: *"Stand by to wear ship."* This command is informational and indicates that the ship is about to wear.

Figure 29. Wearing: Simultaneous Bracing

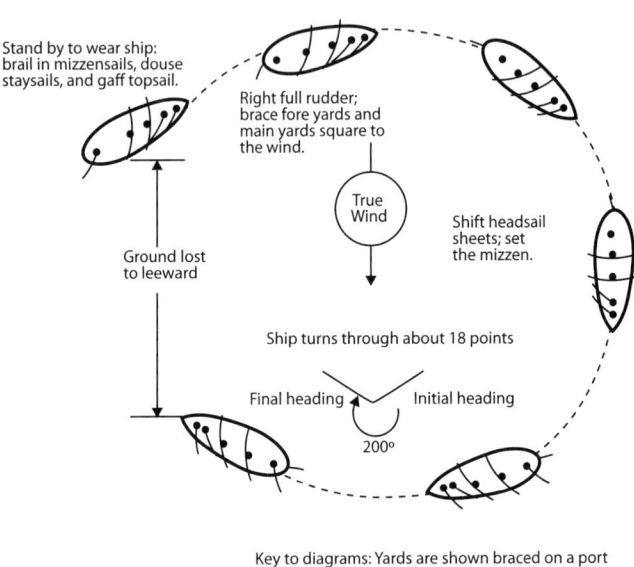

Stand by to wear ship: brail in mizzensails, douse staysails, and gaff topsail.

Right full rudder; brace fore yards and main yards square to the wind.

True Wind

Shift headsail sheets; set the mizzen.

Ground lost to leeward

Ship turns through about 18 points

Final heading   Initial heading

200°

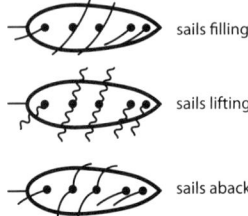

Key to diagrams: Yards are shown braced on a port tack and rudder is shown amidships as an example.

sails filling

sails lifting

sails aback

    d. Mast captain: *"Manned and ready."* To be manned and ready for a wear, all lee gear is taken off the pins and the lee braces are faked out for running. Foremast personnel should man the headsail sheets and the fore braces, tacks, and sheets. Mainmast personnel must douse the main staysails and then man the mainsail gear and main braces before reporting manned and ready. Mizzen personnel must douse the mizzen staysails, brail in the mizzensails, and haul the boom onto the new tack before reporting. The tack jiggers should be cleared away before reporting manned and ready.

    e. OOD to mainmast captain: *"Rise tacks and sheets."* The mainsail is taken in for three reasons: the leads of the tacks and sheets are long and make the mainsail difficult to handle when the yards are braced; taking in the sail gives the OOD a clear view of the entire ship; and, most important, wind is allowed to flow through to the foresails when the ship has turned downwind.

2. Turning off the wind:

    a. OOD: *"Wear-O."* This command is informational, indicating that the wear has begun.

    b. OOD: *"Left (right) full rudder. Brace the yards square to the wind." As* the ship begins to turn, the foremast and mainmast captains give commands to brace the yards to keep them drawing at their best advantage—square to the wind. The ship usually turns slowly, so the actual bracing is often done in stages. The topgallant and royal yards tend to get ahead of the lower yards; hence, the brace captains should ensure that commands are given to keep the yards moving together. Bracing too far will require much more work at the end of the evolution, because the yards will then have to be hauled against the full force of the wind. Mast captains use telltales on their respective masts to keep the yards square to the wind since the relative wind may be slightly different on each mast. Ideally, the main yards should slightly lead the fore yards as they are braced around to maximize the turning moment of the wind.

3. Passing through the wind:
   a. OOD to foremast captain: *"Shift the headsail sheets."* The sheets are shifted to the new tack and trimmed to best advantage as the ship turns back upwind.
   b. OOD to mizzenmast captain: *"Set the mizzensails."* Once set, the mizzensails accelerate the turn of the ship up onto the new course. They do not have to be set, although the turn upwind may take longer without them.

4. Coming up to reach the new course:
   a. OOD: *"Set the mainsail."* This command is given as soon as the yards have been braced to the new tack and the sails are filling properly. As in tacking, this command directs the mast captains to reset the sails that were set prior to the wear, with main and mizzen staysails set first, followed by the mainsail, the mizzensails, and the gaff topsail.
   b. As soon as the ship reaches her new course, the mast captains should trim their sails and fan their yards properly without further command. If the relative wind on the new course is *abeam* or forward of the beam, the fore and main yards should be fanned unless the OOD directs otherwise.

Wearing with a Reduced Crew (Progressive Wearing)

When wearing with the watch section, the procedures are basically the same as when wearing with the full crew, except that the masts are braced separately (see fig. 30). The staysails, mizzensails, gaff topsail, and mainsail are doused prior to commencing the wear. The OOD gives the rudder command and turns the ship to run dead downwind while the main yards are being braced square to the ship. While running downwind, the headsail sheets are shifted and the fore yards are braced around to the new tack. The OOD then turns the ship back up into the wind as the main yards are braced to the new tack. Finally, the mizzen boom is eased onto the new tack and the staysails, mizzensails, gaff topsail, and mainsail are reset.

Bracing the main yards requires careful coordination between the OOD and the boatswain's mate of the watch (BMOW) to ensure that the sails continue drawing and driving the ship.

With a small watch section, the maneuver is time consuming, sometimes lasting an entire watch. A progressive wear should be attempted only when speed and distance are not important considerations. If necessary, the evolution can be completed faster by bracing at the change of the watch, using personnel from both the offgoing and oncoming watch sections.

The commands and procedures for progressive wearing occur in a particular sequence (given below). The commands for progressive wearing are shown in figure 30.

1. Preparatory stage:
    a. OOD: *"Stand by to progressive wear."* This command is informational and indicates that the ship is about to wear.

b. BMOW: *"Manned and ready."* To be manned and ready for progressive wearing, sails are doused in the following order: gaff topsail, upper mizzen, lower mizzen, mizzen staysails, main staysails, and mainsail. All lee gear is taken off the pins, the lee braces are faked out for running, and the fore tack jigger is cleared away. The main braces are then manned before reporting manned and ready.

Figure 30. Wearing: Progressive Bracing

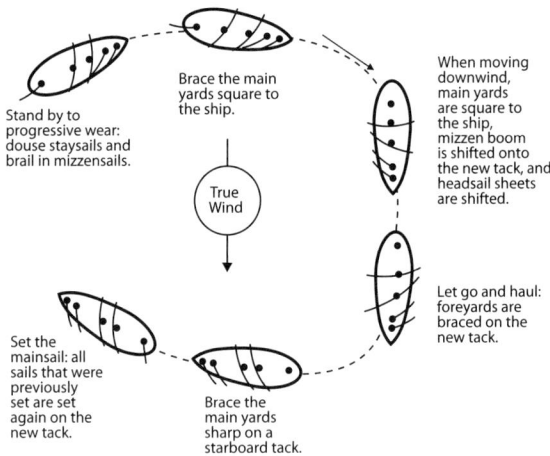

Stand by to progressive wear: douse staysails and brail in mizzensails.

Brace the main yards square to the ship.

When moving downwind, main yards are square to the ship, mizzen boom is shifted onto the new tack, and headsail sheets are shifted.

True Wind

Let go and haul: foreyards are braced on the new tack.

Set the mainsail: all sails that were previously set are set again on the new tack.

Brace the main yards sharp on a starboard tack.

Key to diagrams: Yards are shown braced on a port tack and rudder is shown amidships as an example.

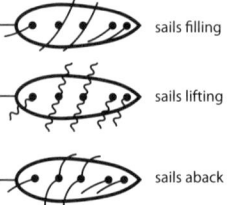

sails filling

sails lifting

sails aback

2. Turning off the wind to run downwind:
    a. OOD: *"Wear-O."* This command is informational, indicating that the wear has begun.
    b. OOD: *"Left (right) full rudder. Brace the main yards square to the ship."*

3. Running before the wind:
    a. OOD: *"Shift the headsail sheets."*
    b. OOD: *"Ease the mizzen boom on the port (starboard) tack."*
    c. OOD: *"Let go and haul."* The fore yards are braced around to the new tack.

4. Coming up to reach the new course:
    a. OOD: *"Left (right) full rudder. Brace the main yards sharp (three points, two points, etc.) on a port (starboard) tack."*
    b. *"Set the mainsail."* This command is given as soon as the yards have been braced to the new tack and the sails are filling properly. As in tacking, this command directs the BMOW to reset the sails that were set prior to the wear, with main and mizzen staysails set first, followed by the mainsail. The mizzensails and gaff topsail are set.
    c. As soon as the ship reaches her new course, the BMOW should trim the sails and fan the yards properly without further command. If the relative wind on the new course is abeam or forward of the beam, the fore and main yards should be fanned unless the OOD directs otherwise.

Boxhauling

Boxhauling is used in crowded anchorages, narrow channels, and other confined waters. Areas such as these make it impossible to *headreach* as far as would be required in tacking and also do not allow for the required room to leeward to wear ship. The evolution combines a tack and a wear, but is more complex and time consuming than either.

The first part of the maneuver is exactly like a tack. The mizzen boom is hauled amidships and the rudder is put over to turn the ship rapidly up into the wind. When the main square sails begin to lift, the command *"Rise tacks and sheets"* is given and, as in tacking, the main and mizzen staysails are doused. Unlike tacking, the mizzensails are brailed in because they are being blanketed by the mainsails and will not be needed in the second half of the evolution. Before the bow comes completely into the wind, the command *"Let go and haul"* is given rather than *"Mainsail haul,"* and the fore yards are *boxed*. When boxed, they rapidly slow the ship. Because they are braced onto the opposite tack, they tend to force the bow back onto the original tack. The ship gains sternway very rapidly and will swing back onto the original tack. As the ship swings, it may be desirable to brace the main yards to the wind so that they do not draw and oppose the braking effect of the fore.

The second part of the evolution begins when the wind has drawn abeam. Both the fore and main yards are braced so that they fill. As the ship sails ahead, a simultaneous wear is carried out. If done correctly, the distance gained upwind during the tacking portion of the maneuver offsets most of the distance normally lost in a wear, so that the ship should end up near where she began—but on the opposite tack.

Figure 31. Boxhauling

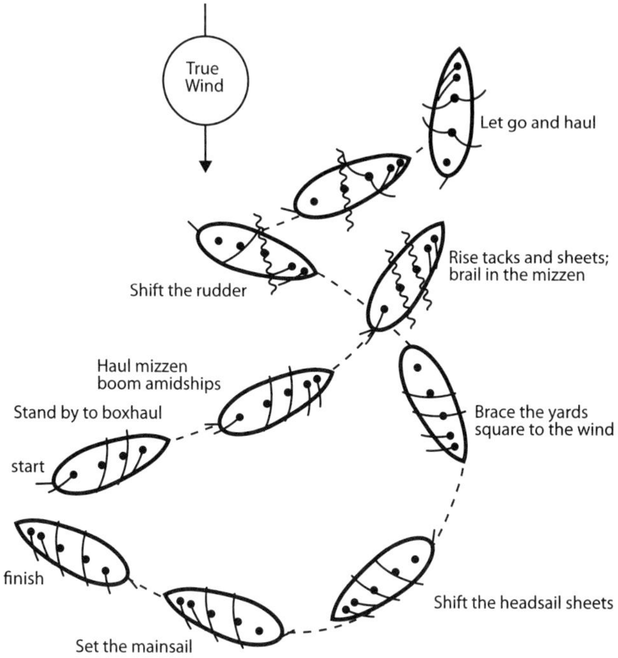

True Wind

Let go and haul

Shift the rudder

Rise tacks and sheets; brail in the mizzen

Haul mizzen boom amidships

Stand by to boxhaul

start

Brace the yards square to the wind

finish

Shift the headsail sheets

Set the mainsail

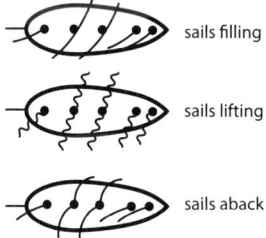

Key to diagrams: Yards are shown braced on a port tack and rudder is shown amidships as an example.

sails filling

sails lifting

sails aback

Eagle is rarely required to boxhaul in confined waters since she has an auxiliary engine available for maneuvering in tight situations. Some of these principles, however, may be put to good use when the ship misses stays while attempting to tack. If the ship comes dead in the water after the main yards have been hauled, the fore and main yards will be boxed and the ship will quickly gather sternway. The rudder is then shifted and the mizzen boom eased or the mizzensails brailed in. Then the headsail sheets are led aft onto the original tack to help force the bow through. The ship should back into the wind with the main square sails eventually filling on the new tack. The command *"Let go and haul"* is given and the headsail sheets are shifted after the bow has come through the wind. The ship will gather headway and then be sailing on the new tack (see fig. 31).

CHAPTER 11

Emergencies

"It appears to me that when an officer takes charge of the deck, his whole mind ought to be occupied with what he would do with the ship in any case of emergency that might take place with the sails that the ship is then under," wrote Captain Learclet of the Royal Navy in 1849. What was true during the Age of Sail remains no less true today. When an emergency strikes, there is rarely enough time to think out a course of action. Solid grounding in navigation and seamanship, forehandedness, and eternal vigilance are absolutely essential for any deck officer while on watch. By anticipating possible emergencies, an officer of the deck (OOD) can avoid most of them and can usually handle the remainder quickly and safely. The sea and wind are ever changing; therefore the proper reaction to any emergency will vary with the circumstances. The OOD must be prepared for an emergency to occur at any time.

Caught Aback

Perhaps the most common sail emergency is being caught aback. This occurs when the square sails back because of a sudden shift of the wind or the inattention of the helmsman or OOD. In light air *Eagle* turns so slowly that it may be impossible to prevent being caught aback by a wind shift. Fortunately, being caught aback in such circumstances is usually more embarrassing than dangerous. In high winds, however, being caught aback can easily result in torn sails and, in extreme conditions, can cause damage to the yards and rigging. Because the ship will rapidly lose headway with the sails backing, quick action is essential to recovery, as is the proper handling of the sails.

Recovery by Boxing Off

The first step in all recovery maneuvers, unless the wind has shifted so far as to make it obvious that the procedure will not work, is to quickly put the rudder over and *fall off* of the wind (see fig. 32a).

If the ship comes dead in the water before the sails refill on the original tack, the fore yards should be boxed by letting go and hauling so that the increased force of the wind backing the fore forces the bow down (see fig. 32b). The mizzensails should be brailed in and, if the ship gains sternway, the rudder must be shifted. When the ship has fallen off enough for the mainsails to fill, the fore yards are braced around again to the original tack so that the ship can gather headway.

Recovery by Hauling Yards

If the wind has shifted around to the original lee bow, and if full rudder has not been successful in bringing the ship around, all hands must be rousted out and sail stations must be set.

If the wind has shifted to the opposite bow the ship has, in essence, tacked unintentionally. If there is no objection to sailing on the new tack, the ship recovers by bracing the yards around as in a normal tack. Tacks and sheets on the mainsail are risen and staysails are doused as soon as possible. On the fore,

Figure 32a. Caught Aback: Falling Off

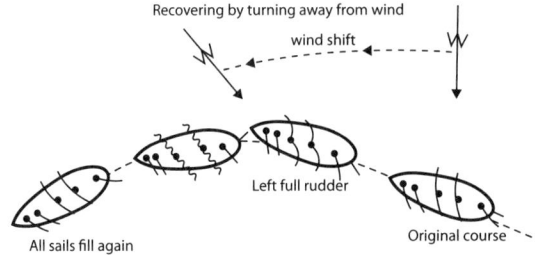

Recovering by turning away from wind

wind shift

Left full rudder

All sails fill again

Original course

Figure 32b. Caught Aback: Boxing Off

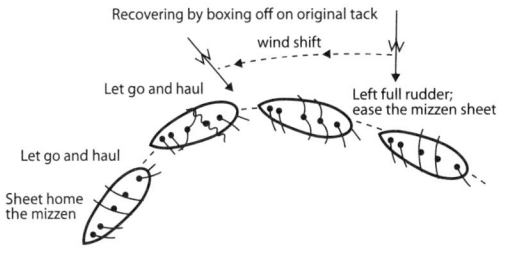

Recovering by boxing off on original tack

wind shift

Let go and haul

Left full rudder;
ease the mizzen sheet

Let go and haul

Sheet home
the mizzen

Figure 32c. Caught Aback: Tacking

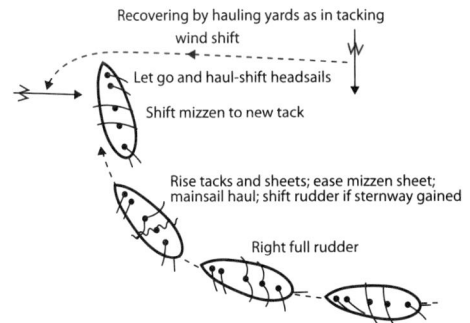

Recovering by hauling yards as in tacking

wind shift

Let go and haul-shift headsails

Shift mizzen to new tack

Rise tacks and sheets; ease mizzen sheet;
mainsail haul; shift rudder if sternway gained

Right full rudder

the headsail sheets are eased or shifted appropriately. The command *"Mainsail haul"* is given and the fore yards are left on the old tack to help swing the bow off onto the new tack. When the mainsails begin to fill, the command *"Let go and haul"* is given. As the ship starts to gather headway, the mainsail, staysails, and mizzensails are set and trimmed for the new tack (see fig. 32c).

Recovery by Chapelling

If for some reason it is necessary to sail on the original tack, the ship may be chapelled (see fig. 33). In *chapelling* the main yards are braced square, the mizzensails brailed in, and the mainsail and staysails doused. The fore, being braced on the original tack, forces the bow down to leeward on the new tack as do the headsails, whose sheets should be held on the original tack so that they back. As the main is squared, *Eagle* will quickly build sternway. As she gains sternway, the rudder is shifted and the ship swings her stern up into the wind.

The mainsails eventually lift and fill, offsetting the backing power of the fore. As the ship gains headway, the rudder is shifted and *Eagle* is wore around onto the original tack, the main being braced to best advantage as the ship turns. The headsail sheets are shifted as the bow passes downwind, and the staysails and mizzensails are then reset.

In chapelling it is particularly important to brail in the mizzensails first to prevent them from holding the bow up into the wind. Once this is done, the ship will come around, although more slowly, even if the main has not been braced square.

As should be evident, chapelling is very similar to boxhauling with the exception that the yards start off on the opposite tack, with the sails aback. In boxhauling, where the purpose is to come about in the least amount of space, the fore yards are braced when' falling off and when wearing, to increase the swing of the ship. Since all three masts are worked, the full crew is needed. By contrast, in chapelling the object is merely to recover on the original tack. Thus, it is sufficient to brail in the mizzensails and,

Figure 33. Caught Aback: Chapelling

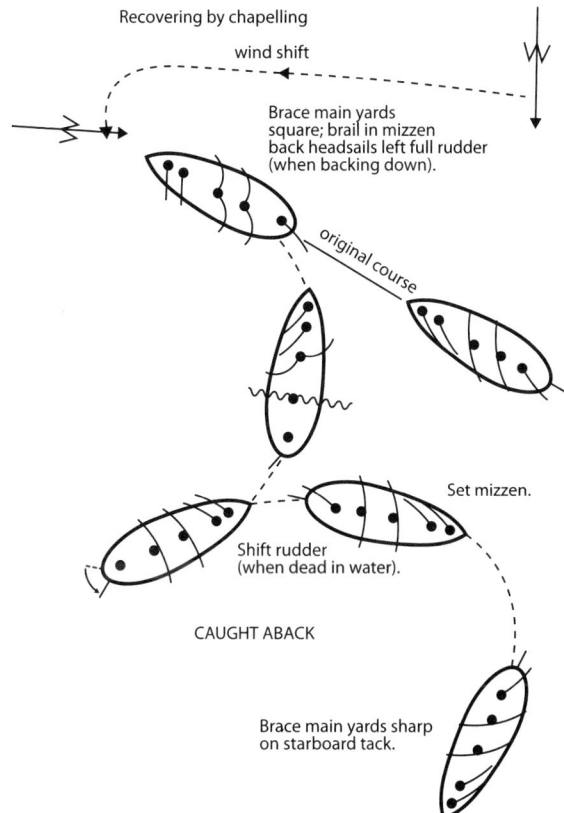

Recovering by chapelling

wind shift

Brace main yards square; brail in mizzen back headsails left full rudder (when backing down).

original course

Set mizzen.

Shift rudder (when dead in water).

CAUGHT ABACK

Brace main yards sharp on starboard tack.

if desired, square the main yards to the ship. This can be done, though with some difficulty, by the watch on deck.

Heavy Weather Sailing

Shortening Sail

Sailing in heavy weather is not in itself dangerous, but it can become so if the OOD and BMOW are not forehanded in anticipating possible problems.

There is sometimes a tendency to keep sails set too long when the weather deteriorates (and, conversely, not to reset them soon enough when the weather improves). In actuality, once the ship's heel exceeds 12 to 15 degrees, the increase of the wetted surface and the additional drag offset much of the extra drive of the wind. Essentially the royals and topgallants are doing more to heel the ship than to drive her. With excessive heel the yards will cockbill beyond the point where the lifts can adjust for the heel, resulting in turbulent wind flow and an additional loss of drive.

Excessive heel may also be dangerous since sudden gusts may heel the ship to the point of endangering the vessel. Additionally, the rudder creates more drag as the ship heels farther over, and, at the same time, it provides less control. In such instances it is often the case that taking in the royals and topgallants and dousing the upper staysails does not appreciably slow the ship. Rather, such shortening is safer and can improve the ride considerably. All in all, the decision to take in sail depends on several factors, including the amount of sea room available, the current and forecasted wind and seas, and the experience level of the crew.

The order of taking in square sails is royals, topgallants, courses, upper topsails, and lower topsails. In heavy weather, sails are normally taken in and furled one at a time on each mast. If they are allowed to slat about in their gear they may tear easily. Thus, topmen are usually stationed in the crosstrees and the tops before the evolution begins so they can lay out onto the yards as soon as each sail is in its gear.

When lowering a movable yard in heavy winds, the yard shoes may bind on their tracks, even when the halyard is slack. Thus, it is important for personnel aloft and mast captains to make sure that the yards are in their fixed lifts before they lay out. Similarly, if there is slack in the braces, the yards may swing violently. The mast captain must ensure that all slack is removed before allowing personnel aloft to furl. The slack created in the braces as the royal and topgallant yards settle into their lifts should be rounded in on the lee side; due to the lead of its braces, however, the upper topsail yard requires rounding in on both sides. Brace captains must ensure that the yards do not slam into the backstays as they come down. In such cases, slack will have to be taken from the weather side.

When furling square sails in heavy weather, the strongest person should lay out to the windward yardarm to smother the leech of the sail. Until the leech is controlled, the wind will continually catch the sail and blow it from the hands of those attempting to furl it. Once the weather leech is controlled, the rest of the sail can be quickly smothered and furled, working from windward to leeward. It may be beneficial for the OOD to pinch up the ship so that the sails begin to lift. This reduces the tendency of the sails to blow away from those furling on the yard. On the other hand, the sails should not be brought aback, in case they blow back on personnel on the yards and possibly knock them from the footropes.

Staysails and headsails are doused by starting with the highest sail and working downward. Usually only a single sail at a time is doused in heavy weather, to prevent slatting and possible tearing. With the staysails, it is particularly important that the sheet be kept under control and that the halyard be eased as rapidly as possible. The sheet should be held to oppose the downhaul until the head of the sail has been hauled down to the miter seam; it must then be eased quickly to fully douse the sail. Careful coordination between halyard, downhaul, and sheet line captains is vital to the success of the evolution. In furling the staysails, sail furlers should work from the top down if there are not enough of them available to furl the entire sail at once. Otherwise the wind may catch the sail and cause it to blow out the lower gaskets.

Extreme Measures: Scudding, Forereaching, and Heaving To

In very heavy weather, a point is reached where the ship cannot make way without pounding into the seas or putting excessive strain on the rigging. If there is sea room in such cases, the ship can *scud* (running directly downwind and down sea under little sail, or *bare poles*). Scudding, however, requires close control to prevent the ship from turning broadside into the trough and *broaching*. When in the trough, the *top-hamper* of the ship and heavy seas may result in dangerous rolling, which at its worst may part rigging or even capsize the ship.

In order to maintain as comfortable a ride as possible in a heavy seaway, while still making progress to windward (or at least not losing ground), the ship may *forereach*—lying to under the main lower topsail braced sharp and the fore-topmast stay-sail *board-sheeted* on the same tack. The helm is tended such that slight lee helm is maintained. Under this sail configuration, *Eagle* will jog slowly over the waves, coming up and falling off with each wave, making slight progress to windward while the crew rests or fixes gear.

If scudding and forereaching are not attempted, the ship may *heave to*, to make the ride as comfortable and safe as possible. In heaving to with the seas on the bow, the main lower topsail or the main-topmast staysail is set on either tack while the fore-topmast staysail is backed on the opposite tack. The OOD may need either to bring the ship into the wind or to head nearly dead downwind in order to set the staysail aback. Finally, the helm is put over all the way to windward and lashed down. Under this configuration *Eagle* will slowly come up into the wind until the main lower topsail (or main-topmast staysail) lifts, and then be blown back to leeward by the backed fore-topmast staysail.

When heaving to with the wind on the quarter, the fore lower topsail should be used to keep the bow well off the wind and a mizzen staysail used to balance the ship and dampen the rolling. In this case much closer rudder control is needed to prevent broaching or allowing the seas to come dead astern, possibly *pooping* the ship.

Eagle may roll heavily, regardless of which heavy weather techniques are used. At times waves may break on deck. Thus, the *heavy weather bill* must be set: lifelines are rigged on deck, heavy weather *gripes* are rigged on the small boats, all loose gear is lashed down, topside personnel don personal floatation devices, and maximum watertight integrity is maintained. Fortunately, the weather is rarely so severe as to require heaving to. When rough weather occurs, however, *Eagle* will ride reasonably well if handled appropriately.

Sailing in or near a Squall

Squalls are associated with the passage of weather fronts and with thunderstorms. In a squall there may be a sudden increase in wind speed—possibly up to hurricane force. Often this increase in speed can be followed by a sudden wind shift of up to 180 degrees within a few minutes or even seconds. This combination of high winds and shifting direction can be extremely dangerous if the ship is under full sail, potentially catching her aback or *knocking her down.*

Squalls can usually be detected both visually and on radar well before they strike. A prudent seaman will fall off and run before a squall. By running, the relative wind speed is reduced by the speed of the ship. Additionally the ship will not heel as much, especially if upper square sails and staysails are set. With the seas and wind astern, sails can be taken in with comparative ease.

Many squalls do not contain high winds, however; if the ship ran off from every one sighted, she would be hard pressed to meet her schedule. Thus, on occasion *Eagle* will be caught before she can fall off or reduce sail. In such a situation the ship will heel excessively. The increased submergence of the lee bow increases its lateral resistance and tends to force the bow up into the wind. Unless quick action is taken on the helm, the ship may get caught aback. In any case an excessive amount of weather helm is needed to maintain course. Moreover, as the ship heels and the rudder becomes less vertical, its turning effect is lessened considerably. Thus, there is little residual helm available for falling off of the wind. Brailing in the mizzensails removes a tremendous force aft of the pivot point as well as lessening the heeling moment, allowing the bow to fall off and the rudder to be eased. An attempt to fall off may not be possible if the mizzensails are not brailed in.

In extremely strong winds, as the wind comes abeam, the heel may increase enough to knock down the ship. In such a case it may be necessary to spill some of wind from the sails by pinching up until the upper sails can be doused. Great care must be taken: the wind must neither be brought too far forward lest the ship be caught aback, nor too far aft lest she be knocked down. Normally the extreme danger will have passed (even in a hurricane-force squall) once the royals, topgallants, and upper staysails have been taken in.

If the ship gets caught with the wind abeam and the heel increases dangerously, as a last resort and only at the direction of the OOD, the sheets for the upper square sails and staysails may be thrown off. This action can tear the sails, but it may save the ship by spilling the wind in those sails that add most to the heel.

The decision to fall off or pinch up must be made according to circumstances; forehandedness and experience on the part of the OOD will ensure the best decision. Obviously the best solution is to avoid the problem, if possible, by falling off and reducing sail before the squall hits. When a squall approaches, it is prudent to fake out the mizzen, royal, and topgallant gear so that they may be handled quickly in an emergency. Additionally, when sailing in areas of known squalls, it is prudent to consider dousing topgallant and royal sails at night.

Gear Failure

Great care is taken in *Eagle* to prevent gear failure. Much of the running rigging is replaced annually; the standing rigging, all blocks, and all fittings are continually inspected and repaired when necessary. Nevertheless, gear failure may occur in heavy weather. The general procedure when gear carries away is to remove the strain from the affected area and to secure the gear from thrashing about so that repairs can be made.

Running Rigging Carries Away

If the **sheet of a square sail** carries away, the sail should be clewed up immediately to prevent it from ripping to shreds. It is not possible to clew down the upper three yards since the clew-line on the affected side will not have any effect in pulling the yard down. Nevertheless, clewing up causes most of the wind to be spilled from the sail. The yard will then normally come down by just easing the halyard once the wind is spilled.

If the **sheet of a headsail or staysail** carries away, the sail should be blanketed by falling off, and it should be doused as quickly as possible. In the case of a mizzen staysail, where the whipping sheet pendant and block may endanger personnel, the halyard should be thrown off even before the downhaul is manned. Providing the ship is running downwind, the force of the wind along the leech should douse the sail.

If the **downhaul** of a headsail or staysail parts, the ship should again fall off. The force of the wind on the leech should be enough to force the sail down, or personnel may be stationed at the tack to pull it down by hand. If the sail jams, a line may be looped around the stay above the sail to pull the head down.

If a weather **brace** should carry away, the yard will fly up against the lee backstays, possibly imparting a dangerous strain on them. The ship should fall off so that some strain is taken by the other brace. The clewlines above and below the yard whose brace has carried away should be kept taut to help control the yard. In marginal conditions where the ship is rolling, it may be beneficial to lash the yard against the backstays until a new brace can be rove.

If the **mizzen sheet** carries away, the boom will slam violently against the mizzen backstays. The preventer should be hauled taut to control the boom and the sails brailed in as soon as possible. If the boom cannot be controlled by the preventer, it should be lashed to the backstays until a new sheet can be rove.

Standing Rigging or Steering Gear Carries Away

If the **bobstay** or any **forward-leading stay** parts, the vessel should be turned downwind to remove all strain. Sail should be reduced if the ship is laboring. A jury (makeshift) stay should be rigged. In the case of the bobstay, a chain can be passed from the end of the bowsprit through the *hawsepipes* and set taut with the capstan.

If a **backstay** or **shroud** parts, the OOD should wear ship immediately to place the strain on the opposite stay. Speed is of the essence because the remaining stays will have to make up for the support of the damaged stay and successive failures may occur. After wearing, a new stay or preventer can be rigged.

If a *truss* or **shoe** carries away, the yard should be braced back and lashed in place. The sails bent and sheeted to it should be taken in before making repairs.

If a **yard** carries away, the lines attached to the spar, such as the sheets, clewlines, braces, and halyard, should be handled in such a way as to minimize the motion of the yard, keeping it from causing more damage. The spar should be temporarily lashed in place to prevent it from causing more damage or crashing to the deck while gear is rigged to lower it. If a spar carries over the side, it should be recovered if possible. If it endangers the ship, it should be cut away immediately.

If there is a **steering casualty** caused by a failure in the linkage between the helm and the rudder, control should be shifted to *after steering*. The *trick wheel* is engaged by pulling the control handle forward to engage the gears. Sound-powered phone talkers should be assigned to relay commands from the bridge. After the casualty has been repaired, it will be necessary to set both the rudder and the *helm indicator* amidships and to line up the gears of the rudder mechanism with those of the main helm before pushing the control aft handle to engage the main helm.

Man Overboard

The cry of "Man overboard" strikes fear in the hearts of all sailors. For a square-rigger, only a well-trained and alert watch will react quickly enough to recover the lost shipmate. Even under power *Eagle* is slower to respond and more difficult to maneuver than modern cutters. Under sail the situation becomes even more difficult, and the entire watch section must always be ready to respond. The officer of the deck is continually reevaluating wind and sea conditions throughout the watch and constantly rehearses the initial action that would be taken for the given conditions. The watch on deck must be properly organized and always ready to lower the boat away expeditiously.

Anyone seeing a crew member go over the side must sing out, *"Man overboard port (starboard) side,"* and then ensure that the report reaches the bridge. Life rings, marker buoys, and marker lights should be thrown to the person. A pipe is immediately made to inform all hands, and the sail stations alarm is sounded. *Eagle* will then be maneuvered to make the quickest and safest pickup possible. Under power, either a shipboard or a small-boat pickup will be made. Under sail, the OOD will order right or left full rudder to bring the ship up into the wind and heave to.

Ships in company are notified by radio and by the use of the *Oscar flag* by day or man overboard lights (rapidly flashing not-under-command lights) by night. If other vessels are nearby, the danger signal should be sounded to alert them and a broadcast made on channel 16. On the bridge and in the combat information center (CIC), the ship's position should immediately be fixed by all means available. The quartermaster of the watch (QMOW) will then report the estimated bearing and range to the person every thirty seconds using a dead reckoning plot and the Global Positioning System (GPS). If the person is in sight, visual bearings should be taken on the bridge and passed to the QMOW so that they can continually update their plot.

The height of eye on *Eagle's* bridge is low enough that the person may be quickly lost visually. The OOD must ensure that the person in the water is kept in sight by having extra personnel don harnesses and lay to the tops and shrouds to point to the person. Similarly, personnel on deck not otherwise engaged should point to the person to help the OOD maintain sight of the person in the water. When maneuvering to recover the person, it is very important that the OOD keep *Eagle* as close to the person as possible and make every effort to maintain visual contact.

Recovery under Power

If under power, the engine may be used to bring the ship back to the vicinity of the person. The approach depends on wind and sea conditions and whether any sails are set. If a shipboard pickup is made, the vessel should be maneuvered to stop the ship slightly upwind of the person. Although there are a number of ways to maneuver in a man overboard situation, there are three basic options under power.

1. *Modified destroyer, or "racetrack," turn.* This type of pickup involves coming around a full 360 degrees, stopping upwind, and then drifting down on the person. With a single rudder and single screw, *Eagle* does not have a tight-enough turning radius to complete a regular destroyer turn and return to the person in the water. Thus, it is important that the rudder be brought amidships for a brief period midway through the turn to ensure that a proper approach can be made. The OOD must be careful not to travel any farther from the person than necessary to be able to make the pickup. A boat may be lowered when the ship nears the person or a shipboard pickup can be made. In any case a pipe should be made informing all hands as to the side and type of pickup.

2. *Williamson turn.* In low visibility or at night, the Williamson turn is generally preferred. The rudder is put over full in the direction of the person, but it is shifted once the ship's head has swung 60 degrees. This type of turn is also used when the OOD is unsure when the person was lost. *Eagle* should return to a reciprocal of her own track, and lookouts are stationed to look and listen for the missing person. A Williamson turn has the disadvantage of taking longer than a modified destroyer turn, and it also carries the ship much farther away.

3. *Back down.* As already mentioned, *Eagle* does not turn as quickly as most cutters. Therefore, it is sometimes best for the

OOD to order *"Right (left) full rudder"* to help swing the stern clear of the person and *"Engine back full"* at the same time. The stern will swing clear of the person, and by the time the engine responds with astern turns, the person will be well clear of the screw. If the watch is alert and responds quickly, it will be possible to stop *Eagle* close enough to keep the person in sight. The small boat is immediately lowered and directed to make the pickup. This method is most effective when the ship is steaming at a standard bell or less in benign wind and sea conditions, but it can be used at any time.

Recovery under Sail Alone

If under sail alone, the ship should be brought up into the wind (but not through) to slow headway to 2 to 4 knots, so that the small boat can be launched. After giving the helm command (left/right rudder) to bring the ship up into the wind, the OOD should concentrate on lowering the boat and keeping the person in sight. As the full crew arrives on deck, another OOD can help with the sail-handling commands.

When sufficient personnel have arrived on deck to handle sail and the small boat is away, the command *"Let go and haul"* should be given to box the fore and main yards. Although the command *"Mainsail haul"* will also stop the vessel and bring her to, it is an almost impossible command to execute while lowering the small boat since the mainsail sheets, main braces, and timenoguy are all inaccessible.

"Let go and haul," on the other hand, is a command that can be executed quickly using personnel from both the foremast and the mainmast while not interfering with the critical boat-lowering operation. It is most important that the yards be

boxed and *Eagle* stop her headway, so that she will remain as close as possible to the person in the water and that the small boat may be recovered as soon as possible.

After the fore yards have been braced, sails can be doused or trimmed as necessary. In coming up into the wind, the OOD should attempt to keep the bow from coming through the wind. As long as the vessel does not come head to wind a lee will be provided for the small boat. Once the yards are boxed, the ship will lie to with the fore backing and the main drawing, and drift slowly downwind. The OOD should never turn downwind unless the ship would be endangered by being caught aback. Turning downwind will quickly carry *Eagle* away from the person in the water, and the ship could not be stopped without dousing all sail.

Whenever under sail, sail handling is done by personnel arriving on deck. The watch is completely engaged in lowering the boat away and the actual recovery of the person. As soon as the pipe "Man overboard" is made, the engine room should immediately bring the main engine on the line and be prepared to answer bells as soon as possible. In an emergency, the main engine may be the most effective means of maneuvering the ship and lowering the small boat, even under sail.

Recovery while Motorsailing

If *Eagle* is motorsailing, a careful judgment of circumstances must be made. In light winds or with only fore-and-aft sails set, it may be possible to make a shipboard pickup by using the engine to force the bow through the wind. In moderate winds it will probably be necessary to handle sails much as if the ship were under sail alone. The actual method used when motorsailing depends on the wind and sea conditions, as well as the sails set when the person goes overboard. Backing down and lowering a boat may be an option even with sails set.

Collision Avoidance

So few square-rigged vessels remain afloat that meeting one at sea is something of a rarity, and as a result many power-driven vessels sighting one will come in for a closer look. This is not necessarily dangerous, but since *Eagle* is not easily maneuvered under sail or power, the OOD must always be prepared to take action to avoid a close-quarters situation. As with any cutter, a sharp lookout must be maintained at all times. A record of visual bearings and a careful radar plot should be maintained for all contacts to determine if risk of collision exists.

If risk of collision does exist, communications should be attempted on VHF-FM channel 16 (and channel 13 in U.S. coastal waters). When calling, the OOD should ensure that the other vessel understands that *Eagle* is a sailing vessel. Identifying the ship as "United States Coast Guard sailing ship *Eagle*" or "United States Coast Guard tall ship *Eagle*" generally works well. If communications cannot be established to make a safe passing arrangement, the OOD may need to take action in accordance with the "Rules of the Road" (*Navigation Rules [International-Inland]*, COMDTINST 16672.2D) and the commanding officer's standing orders to the officer of the deck.

Under Power

Collision avoidance while under power is similar to that for any cutter. With relatively low power and a single screw, however, action should be taken earlier, and changes in course and speed must be obvious to the other vessel. When under both sail and power, the OOD should remember that *Eagle* is considered a power-driven vessel and should display the appropriate navigational lights or day shape.

Under Sail Alone

When *Eagle* is under sail alone, power-driven vessels must stay clear of her. Unfortunately not all vessels will recognize *Eagle* as a sailing vessel, particularly at night. First, it is more difficult to see a sailing vessel since she displays no white lights forward, and the red and green lights cannot be seen as far. Second, it is more difficult to determine *Eagle*'s aspect since there are no *masthead* lights, and sidelights are the only indication another vessel will have as to her target angle. Also, in good winds, the heel of the ship may obscure the visibility of the leeward sidelight. Therefore, the OOD must do everything possible to make *Eagle* identifiable. Early radiotelephone calls, proper signal broadcasting over the Automatic Identification System (AIS) and other bridge equipment, and illumination of sails with the sail floodlights can all help avoid close-quarters situations.

Since the maneuvering options open to the OOD under sail are quite limited compared to those of a power-driven vessel, early action is particularly important to avoid a close-quarters situation. Increasing or decreasing speed by setting or taking in sail takes valuable time and thus is generally not an option as it would be on a power-driven vessel. Most often, the OOD will want to turn into the wind or fall off to avoid the other vessel. Again, the OOD should always remember that it is more difficult to detect *Eagle*'s changes in aspect since there are no masthead lights. Therefore, when maneuvering, action not only must be taken early but also must be substantial.

Sail balance should also be considered before deciding to turn. When falling off, the mizzensails may have to be brailed in; keep in mind, however, that falling off may actually increase *Eagle*'s speed. Pinching up into the wind, on the other hand, both alters course and slows the ship.

Another option available is to order a full rudder turn into the wind and stop the ship by intentionally being caught aback. When under sail, this is the only way to stop the ship. This should be done only when there is no other safe way to avoid the other vessel, however, since it means having to call all hands on deck and also virtually eliminates any further maneuvering to avoid the other vessel.

Having the engine on the line is one of the safest ways to avoid endangering the ship, and it should be used if necessary. Although not normally done, the engine may be put on line in five minutes or less in emergency situations. Therefore, an early decision must be made as to whether to order it lit off.

Great care must be taken to quickly identify the applicable "Rules of the Road" situation. For example, the most dangerous situation for *Eagle* often occurs when a power-driven vessel located on the starboard bow is on a collision course. In this case, if the master of the power-driven vessel does not recognize *Eagle* as a sailing ship, she or he will assume *Eagle* must give way. Often this error is not caught until late in the maneuvering situation, particularly at night.

Minimizing Collision Damage

No one likes to think of collision, but forehanded evaluation of the possibilities can minimize the damage. Obviously, if at all possible, collision should be avoided. If action to avoid a collision has been unsuccessful or if the OOD is uncertain as to the intentions of the other vessel, the danger signal must be sounded. If a collision becomes imminent, the collision alarm must be sounded and the highest state of material readiness condition (ZEBRA) set. How the ship is maneuvered depends on wind and sea conditions, as well as on the relative size and maneuverability of the two vessels.

The large size of *Eagle*'s compartments, the limited number of watertight bulkheads, and the location of the largest berthing areas amidships make it particularly important that *Eagle* not be hit broadside. In general *Eagle* should be turned to reduce the relative speed between the two ships as much as possible so that a sideswipe, rather than a head-on collision, occurs. As a last resort it may be preferable to turn into the oncoming vessel and attempt a bow-on approach. The bowsprit will absorb much of the force of a collision and, hopefully, will limit most of the damage to areas above the waterline. In all cases, decisions while in extremis should be made to avoid being hit broadside.

GLOSSARY

Note: Terms enclosed by quotation marks are used as commands.

aback. A sail is aback when the wind strikes it on the forward side; this can be intentional in maneuvering or unexpected in a sudden wind shift.

abeam. A direction away from either side of a vessel (90 degrees or 270 degrees relative to the ship's heading).

after steering. The emergency steering station located on the fantail that is engaged if there is a casualty to the main steering station on the bridge.

amidships. The portion of a vessel midway between the bow and stern or midway between the port and starboard sides.

anemometer. An instrument used to measure the direction and speed of the wind. The sensor for the anemometer is located on the mizzenmast. The anemometer gives the relative wind direction and speed.

astern. A direction behind a vessel (180 degrees relative to the ship's heading).

"Avast." Immediately stop executing the last command and hold what you have. Do not belay until directed. Used only when continuing will endanger gear or personnel. The normal command would be **"That's well."**

back. (1) In the Northern Hemisphere, a change in the wind direction in a counterclockwise direction.(2) Intentionally causing the sails to be aback, as in tacking. (3) To reverse the direction of the ship (i.e., gain sternway).

"Back easy." Slowly ease the line, either to check a stopper or to take turns on or off a belaying pin.

backstay. Standing rigging leading from a point on the mast to the rail abaft the mast.

bagpipe. Backing the lower mizzen by hauling it amidships and then to windward using the weather preventer, to create a greater turning moment. Sometimes used when tacking in light air.

bare poles. A description of a sailing vessel with all sail taken in. Running under bare poles is an extreme heavy weather technique used when carrying sail is dangerous or impractical.

barque. A sailing vessel with three or more masts whose after mast is fore-and-aft rigged. Note: *Eagle* is not a *ship.* She is called one only for convenience in this manual. A *ship* is square-rigged on all masts.

barquentine. A sailing vessel with three or more masts whose foremast is square-rigged and after masts are rigged fore and aft.

"Belay." Secure a line to a belaying pin, cleat, or other point established for this purpose.

bend. (1) To fasten a sail securely to the jackstay on a yard by means of robands. (2) A method of fastening one line to another.

bending shot. A length of chain, with a swivel approximately one fathom in length, that connects the anchor to the first shot of anchor chain. Also known as the *swivel shot.*

binnacle. The wooden housing for the ship's magnetic steering compass.

blanket. A sail is blanketed when the wind is prevented from striking it, either by another vessel passing close aboard to weather or by the sails on another mast on the same ship.

board sheeting. Taking all possible slack out of a headsail or staysail sheet.

"Board the tack." Secure a special tackle called the **tack jigger** to the weather clew of the foresail or mainsail and haul it down to the rail. Used when sailing by the wind (close-hauled).

bobstay. A heavy stay (a steel rod on *Eagle*) running from the stem of the ship to the end of the bowsprit. Provides support for the bowsprit.

boltrope. Roping around the edges of a sail. See also **tabling**.

boom. (1) A spar used to support the foot of the lower or upper mizzen. (2) A spar used to extend the reach of a line for handling cargo or in mooring boats, as in the cargo boom and boat boom.

bottles. See **turnbuckle**.

bowsprit. The large spar on the bow of a sailing vessel. Provides a good lead for the stays that support the mast and the headsails.

boxhauling. Sailing maneuver for changing tacks that is used in confined waters when there is not sea room to tack and the loss of ground in wearing is unacceptable.

boxing. A maneuver that can be used when caught aback if the wind is still on the weather bow. The fore and main yards are braced on opposite tacks, providing enough force to push the bow off the wind; also used in man overboard situations or to slow the ship when heaving to.

braced sharp. Yards braced so that they make an angle of approximately 45 degrees (four points) to the centerline of the ship.

braced square. Yards braced so that they are perpendicular to the heading of the ship.

braces. Lines used to move the yards in a horizontal plane.

bracing. Swinging the yards in a horizontal plane.

brailing in. Dousing the lower or upper mizzensails.

brails. Lines used to haul in the lower and upper mizzen to the mast when dousing.

broach. To be thrown broadside to a heavy surf or sea.

bull's eye. Circular piece of hardwood or nylon hollowed in the center. Has a groove around it for a strop and a hole for the lead of a line. Used to change the lead of a line where a block is not required.

bumpkins. Steel supports extending outboard from the sides of a square-rigger to support blocks for the braces and to lead them clear of the ship.

bunt-leechlines. Lines on the square sails used to furl the square sails by bringing the leech and foot up to the yard.

buntlines. Lines used to douse a square sail that haul the foot up to the yard.

by the wind. Close-hauled, or sailing as close to the wind as possible. *Eagle* can sail approximately 75 to 80 degrees from the **true wind**.

cap. A band at the head of the mast. In older sailing vessels the cap held the lower part of the topmasts to the lower masts.

carry away. To fail or to break loose, as in lines parting, sails tearing, or spars coming unhoused as a result of excessive strain.

cast or casting. To swing the vessel's head as necessary when maneuvering under power. Also called *back and fill*.

catenary. A dip in a line or chain caused by the weight of the line itself. The catenary provides a spring or elastic effect.

caught aback. The ship is caught aback when, because of a wind shift or helmsman error, the wind strikes the forward rather than the after side of the square sails.

chafing. The wearing down of ropes, lines, sails, or other parts of the ship by the rubbing action caused by the ship's motion or wind.

chapelling. A recovery maneuver used when caught aback and the wind has shifted to the opposite bow; the main yards are braced square to the ship, the stern is backed into the wind, and the ship is wore around.

cheek blocks. Blocks attached to the yardarms through which square sail sheets are led.

"Clear away." Lay out a coil so that the line will run freely. Applies to downhauls, weather staysail sheets, and so on. Also used to refer to striking the tack jigger.

clew. The lower corners of a square sail or the after lower corner of a fore-and-aft sail.

"Clew down." Haul on the clewlines while holding the sheets in order to settle a yard into its fixed lifts.

"Clew up." Haul on clewlines, buntlines, and bunt-leechlines until the sail is gathered in its gear below the yard.

clew-garnet. Special term for the clewlines of the foresail and mainsail.

clewlines. Lines that lead upward from the clews of the upper four square sails to the yards above and thence to the pinrails. Clewlines oppose sheets, and are used for dousing square sails. Courses have **clew-garnets** rather than clewlines.

close-hauled. Point of sail where a vessel is sailing as near to the wind as possible. See also **full and by** and **by the wind**.

cockbill. Yards are cockbilled when they are canted with respect to the horizontal. When in their lifts, the upper yards will cockbill when braced sharp. When sails are set, cockbill is adjusted by the fore and main lifts. Cockbill can only be removed in the upper three yards when sails are set.

come-along. A chain or wire tackle with a ratchet mechanism used to lift or take a strain as the ratchet is engaged.

courses. Collective term for both the mainsail and foresail.

crane lines. Athwartship lines or wire rope for personnel to work between the shrouds; similar to **ratlines**.

cringle. Ring or grommet worked into the tabling of a sail at the head, clew, or leech. Used to make lines or rope fast.

crosstrees. Platform aloft located where the topmast and top-gallant mast come together.

deadman. An improperly furled section of a sail that looks as if a dead man could be furled inside it.

dograil. The first timbers on either side of the stem, form-ing the seat of the bowsprit. On board *Eagle*, the headsail downhauls are belayed to pins on the dograil. Sometimes called *knightshead*.

dolphin striker. A strut or brace extending almost vertically downward from the bowsprit to the bobstay.

douse. To take in a sail.

downhaul. A line used for dousing a headsail or staysail that is led from the deck through the head of the sail to the clew.

earing. A short piece of line secured to a cringle used to make fast. For hauling out the upper corners of the head of a square sail when bending it to its yard.

"Ease." Pay out slowly and with care; reduce strain on the line.

fairlead. A block or fitting that changes the direction (lead) of a line without giving mechanical advantage, or that allows it to run free without chafing (fair).

fairlead board. A board with holes in it for running rigging to pass through.

fall off. When a sailing vessel changes course in a direction away from the wind.

falls. The line in a tackle that is rove through the blocks to create a mechanical advantage.

fanning. Bracing the weather yardarms slightly aft for each yard as you go higher. Used to take advantage of the differences in relative wind speeds at different altitudes off the water.

fid. A wooden **marlinspike** (pointed tool to separate strands of rope) used primarily to splice line but also used to secure a sea painter to a small boat.

fife rail. A rail around three sides of each mast, used to belay running rigging.

flemish horse. A footrope at the tip of a yard.

flukes. The broad flat sections of the anchor that actually dig into the bottom. The flukes can rotate on the anchor stock. Occasionally when the anchor is weighed, the flukes will point in toward the hull and will have to be tripped or rotated so the anchor may be hawsed.

following sea. A sea running in the same direction as the ship's course.

foot. The lower edge of a sail.

footropes. Ropes that hang below a yard to provide footing for personnel who must climb out on a yard and handle sail.

forereach. Configuring the ship to ride slowly through heavy seas, setting the main lower topsail braced sharp and the fore-topmast staysail board-sheeted, both on the same tack.

freeing ports. Openings in the side of a ship to carry off seawater that has come over the rail.

full and by. Sailing as close to the wind as possible with all sails drawing full and course changes being made to adjust for wind shifts. Sailing full and by allows the vessel to make as much ground to weather as possible without pinching. With all sails set, *Eagle* can sail about 75 degrees off the true wind when sailing full and by.

furl. To take in a sail and secure it. See also **harbor furl** and **sea furl**.

futtock shrouds. Steel rods leading from the futtock band below the tops to the edge of the tops, providing a foundation for the topmast shrouds.

gaff. A spar on the mizzen used for extending the head of the lower or upper mizzen.

gallows frame. The teak-planked steel frame that spans from the boat deck to the gunwale athwartships of the laundry space.

gantline. A whip (purchase) rigged aloft for general utility purposes.

gasket. Line or canvas strap used to secure a sail when furled.

goosewing. To set only the leeward side of a sail. Chafing gear may be passed around the sail at the center of the yard and the weather side remains in its gear. The mainsail may be goosewinged to prevent blanketing the foresail and the maintopmast staysail when sailing with the wind abaft the beam.

gripe. Fastenings for securing a ship's boat in its cradle or to the rail.

halyard. Line used for hoisting and lowering sails and yards.

"Hand over hand." Haul on a line using one hand then the other, never losing contact or control of the line.

"Handsomely." Execute a command deliberately and carefully but not necessarily slowly.

hank. Circular metal fitting that rides on a stay and to which the luff of a staysail is seized.

harbor furl. To furl a sail methodically to ensure a uniform and neat appearance, as is done before a high-visibility port visit. See also **sea furl.**

haul. (1) In the Northern Hemisphere, a shift in the wind in a clockwise direction. Also called **veer**. (2) To pull without the aid of machinery.

hawsepipes. Heavy castings through which anchor chain runs from the wildcat through the deck to the anchor.

head. The top edge of a square sail that is bent to the yard. On a fore-and-aft sail, the halyard is secured to the head.

header. A temporary shift in wind direction requiring a vessel to fall off.

headreach. The distance the ship travels forward while tacking.

"Heave around." Haul on a line with the aid of machinery such as a capstan or winch.

heave to (under sail). To stop the ship's headway by turning into the wind or by backing the sails on one or more masts.

heavy weather bill. A procedure that readies the ship for riding out a storm. The bill requires rigging lifelines, lashing down loose gear, and setting maximum conditions of material and engineering readiness.

helm indicator. A dial located on the helm stand that indicates how many degrees the helm has been turned. The rudder angle indicator, located on the stack, shows how many degrees the rudder has actually moved.

"Helm's alee." Informational command to indicate that a tacking maneuver has begun.

"Hold." Do not allow the line to be eased; hold until the line parts.

house. To lower the fore and main topgallant masts so that *Eagle* may pass safely under a bridge. The topgallant masts can be lowered approximately thirteen feet.

in irons. A vessel is in irons when it stops during a tack with the wind dead ahead and cannot be turned either way.

in its gear. When a sail has been taken in and is being held by its gear: buntlines, leechlines, bunt-leechlines, and clewlines all two-blocked and belayed.

in its lifts. A yard is in its lifts when the halyard has been eased and the yard hauled down so that its entire weight is supported by the fixed lifts.

inhaul. A line used to haul the head and foot of a mizzensail into the mast. Inhauls are employed when dousing the mizzensails.

Irish pennant. Any piece of loose line or gear adrift in the rigging.

jackstay. A metal rod to which sails or lines are secured, located on top of a yard on the forward side.

jibe. A maneuver for a sailing vessel to change tacks by bringing the stern through the wind. Fore-and-aft-rigged vessels jibe, whereas square-riggers *wear*, which is another term for a controlled jibe.

jigger. A purchase generally used to take additional strain on running rigging.

knightshead. See **dograil**.

knockdown. To cause sudden and extreme heeling, as from a strong gust of wind. When a sailing ship is heeled over so far that the yardarms enter the water, she is said to have been *knocked down*, or *laid on her beam ends*.

lanyard. Any piece of small, strong line used to secure accessories to one's person while going aloft.

leather. A short strip of leather tucked into the braces after they have stretched out to mark where the yards are braced square or sharp.

lee. Away from the direction of the wind. Objects on that side are said to be to **leeward** (downwind).

lee helm. A condition where there is too much force from the sails forward of the pivot point, causing the ship to fall off the wind, which must be corrected for by turning the rudder to weather to steer a straight course. Lee helm is often a symptom of inadequate sail trim or balance.

leech. The after edge of a fore-and-aft sail or the sides of a square sail.

leechlines. Lines leading to the leeches of a square sail that haul them up to the yards for furling.

leeward. Direction away from the wind (downwind).

leeway. Drift of a vessel or other floating object to **leeward** (downwind).

"Let go and haul." Brace the yards of the foremast to the opposite tack when maneuvering under sail.

lift. (1) A lesser degree of luffing on the square sails, when the wind is almost parallel to the yards, striking along the leeches, causing them to shiver rather than fill. (2) A temporary shift in the wind allowing the vessel to turn toward the direction of the wind.

lifts. Fixed lifts are rigged on the royal, topgallant, and upper topsail yards to keep them secure when fully lowered. Adjustable lifts are rigged on the fore and main yards to permit moving yards in a vertical plane as required.

line. In general, sailors refer to fiber rope as line; wire rope is referred to as *rope*, *wire rope*, or just *wire*.

"Lively." Execute the command quickly, either easing or hauling at a faster pace.

lizard. A short length of line having a thimble (or thimbles) spliced into its ends. Used as a leader for rigging.

luff. (1) The leading edge of a fore-and-aft sail. (2) The shake or slat of a sail when the sheet is too slack or the vessel is too close to the wind.

"Mainsail haul." Brace the yards of the mainmast to the opposite tack when maneuvering under sail.

"Man." Station sufficient personnel to handle a line, considering its purpose and weather conditions.

manned and ready. A line is manned and ready when there are enough people to work the line properly and enough turns have been cleared off the pin so the line may be worked.

marlinspike. A tool used in rope work primarily to assist in untying knots, unlaying line for splicing, or other tasks.

marry. To twist together two or more lines so that the friction between them will prevent the lines from running free.

Lines are married to allow them to be belayed safely when a stopper is not being used.

martingale stay. The stay that runs from the dolphin striker to the stem of the ship. Provides support for the dolphin striker and bowsprit.

masthead. The top of a lower mast where the foretop or maintop is situated.

miter seam. The seam of a headsail or staysail that leads from the clew to the luff.

mizzen sheet. A threefold **purchase** that leads from padeyes on the fantail to the end of the mizzen boom; used to control the boom.

monkey rails. Two rails on the forecastle used to belay the headsail sheets.

off the wind. When the ship is not sailing close-hauled and the true wind is abaft the beam.

Oscar flag. A square red and yellow code flag that represents the letter "O."

outhaul. Line used to haul out the head or the foot of the lower or upper mizzen.

overhaul. To place slack in clewlines, buntlines, bunt-leechlines, and associated tackle when sails are set to ensure efficient sail shape is maintained in buntlines, leechlines, and so on.

padeye. Steel ring welded to a deck or bulkhead to which gear is rigged.

peak. The aft upper corner of a mizzensail.

pinch. To sail a ship or boat too close to the wind so that the sails lose their maximum driving power, thus causing the vessel to slow or stall. A vessel can be *pinching* without the sails luffing.

pinrail. A strong wooden rail or bar with holes through it to hold belaying pins, which are in turn used for belaying (securing) lines.

point. One of thirty-two divisions of a compass card. One point corresponds to 11.25 degrees. *Pointing* can refer to a sailing vessel's course and ability to steer close to the wind.

pooped. A vessel is pooped when a heavy sea breaks over the stern or quarter. Usually occurs when running before the wind in a gale.

preventer. A line or tackle used to provide extra safety. The most common preventer on *Eagle* is used to prevent the mizzen boom from jibing.

purchase. A general term for a mechanical arrangement of blocks and line for multiplying force, often classified by its mechanical advantage. A *twofold purchase* (also known as a *double tackle*), consisting of two double blocks and four falls (lines between blocks), has a four-to-one advantage. A *threefold purchase* (two treble blocks and six falls) has a six-to-one advantage.

quarter. A position 45 degrees abaft either beam; directly between **abeam** and **astern**.

rake. The fore/aft trim of a mast. Masts are designed to be raked differently on various classes of ships. On board *Eagle*, each mast has a slight aft rake; when viewed from the side, the top of the mast is aft of the base.

ratlines. Lines seized to the shrouds upon which personnel climb to lay aloft.

rattail jigger. A light purchase with a stopper shackled to the becket of a block. Used to sweat down lines by passing the stopper around the line and hauling it down to the deck.

reach. The points of sail when a sailing vessel is neither beating to windward nor running before the wind.

"Ready about." A preparatory command given by the officer of the deck for personnel to man and ready lines and equipment necessary to tack *Eagle*.

relative wind. The wind *Eagle*'s anemometer indicates is the combination of the **true wind** and the variation to it caused by the vessel's motion through the water. The wind that is felt by an observer on board a moving vessel, measured in degrees relative.

"Rise tacks and sheets." Clew up the mainsail when maneuvering under sail. This command is also used to direct personnel to douse the staysails in a tack.

roband. Short length of marline used to secure the head of a square sail to the jackstay or the luff of a headsail to the hanks.

rope. In the maritime services, rope is wire cordage. If made of fiber, it is referred to as **line**.

rotten stuff. Any of a variety of small yarns, usually salvaged from old lines, used to stop off gear. Rotten stuff must be strong enough to hold the gear but light enough to break easily when tugged.

"Round in." Bring the blocks of a tackle together by hauling on the line.

running rigging. Movable lines and blocks used for handling sails, yards, and so on.

safety stay. The aftermost of the two jackstays on each yard. It is so called because it provides a handhold (and a point of attachment for safety belt hooks) for personnel working on the yards.

scallops. Slack sections of the luff of a fore-and-aft sail caused by not properly hauling on the halyard when setting the sail. Scallops create turbulence and should be removed.

Scotchman. Wooden batten fastened to the standing rigging to prevent chafing.

scud. To run before the wind in heavy weather with reduced sail, such as the main lower topsail and the foresail.

scupper. A drain in the deck to carry off the accumulation of rain or seawater from the waterways.

sea furl. To furl a sail rapidly without concern for its appearance. See also **harbor furl**.

sea painter. Line used to make fast a boat's bow to a ship.

seize. To fasten ropes together by turns of small stuff.

set. To maneuver sails into position such that they provide a propulsive force to *Eagle*.

shaft alley. The compartment aft of the engine room through which the propeller shaft runs.

sheet. Running rigging secured to the clew of a sail (opposing the clewline).

"Sheet home." Ease the clewlines, buntlines, and leechlines, and haul on the sheets until only a few links of the sheet chain remain above the sheet block. Used when setting square sails. This command is also given to personnel on headsails and staysails to haul the sheet in and trim it to best advantage.

ship. A sailing vessel with three or more masts that is square-rigged on all masts. (*Eagle* is technically not a ship. See **barque**.)

shoe. A fitting at the center of the upper three yards that rides in a track bolted to the mast and secures the yard to the mast.

shrouds. Standing rigging used to support a mast laterally, led athwartships from aloft to the deck.

"Slack." Pay out fairly rapidly; remove all of the strain from the line.

slatting about. Moving uncontrollably as sheets, yards, or blocks may do in a sailing evolution if not watched closely.

slot. The space between two headsails or staysails. The width of the slot should be adjusted by use of the sheets to create the fastest airflow, which will then increase the driving power of the sails.

small stuff. Small cordage designated by the number of threads or by special names such as marline.

spar. (1) A wooden or hollow steel cylinder, used aboard sailing vessels as masts, yards, gaffs, or booms. (2) A pale wood color, yellowish-beige in appearance.

spider band. A metal band just above the deck on each mast, with fittings on which miscellaneous gear can be stowed.

spreader. Extension projecting horizontally at the crosstrees to spread backstays.

stacked. The yards are stacked when each is parallel to and aligned with the yard immediately below it.

"Stand by to wear ship." An informational command issued by the officer of the deck for all hands to man and ready lines and equipment necessary to wear *Eagle*.

standing part. The fixed part of any piece of running rigging; the end that is permanently secured.

standing rigging. Wire rope or steel rigging that serves to support the masts in place; it generally does not move and is painted black, white, or spar.

stays. (1) The standing rigging that is the fore-and-aft support for the masts; some stays carry staysails. (2) An alternate term for **tacking**. The ship is in stays while coming through the wind and misses stays when she does not make it through the wind.

step. Masts are *stepped on* (rest on) secure foundations on the keel or the lower decks. The topgallant masts must be *stepped* (raised) after they have been *housed* (lowered) to go under a bridge.

steering casualty. A shipboard emergency in which, for whatever reason, the rudder cannot be controlled from the bridge.

stirrups. Wire rope pendants that are seized to the safety stays and are used to support the footropes.

stopper. A short length of line fixed to the deck, used to hold a line under strain while it is being belayed.

strop. A rope spliced into a circle for use around the shell of a block or bull's eye (as in a lizard).

tabling. A broad hem of extra canvas or dacron sewn into the edges of sails to reinforce them. Serves the same purpose as the **boltrope** used on older sails.

tack. (1) Lines leading forward from the clew of the courses. (2) The lower forward corner of a fore-and-aft sail.

tacking. A sailing maneuver: the process of bringing the ship's bow through the wind to get the wind on the opposite side.

tack jigger. A tackle used to haul down the weather tack of the foresail or mainsail.

telltale. Any flag or pennant that gives an indication of the relative wind.

"Tend." Monitor a line to ensure that neither too much slack nor too much tension is placed on that line as it moves during a sail-handling evolution.

"That's well." Command used to indicate that a line has been hauled enough. A milder form of the command **"Avast."**

throat. The forward upper corner of a mizzensail.

"Throw off." Take a line off the pin and see that the line runs freely. This command never applies to lines under a heavy strain, except in emergencies.

timenoguy. Pronounced "tim-en-ah-gee." Lines used to support a long and heavy line such as the main braces on *Eagle*. The timenoguy prevents the main braces from fouling on the small boat davits when bracing around.

top. (1) The first platform on the foremast and the mainmast—i.e., the "foretop" and the "maintop." Not the actual highest point of the mast. (2) To haul on a topping lift to hoist the cargo boom.

top-hamper. The collective term for all yards, rigging, and gear above the deck that resist the wind.

topmen. Personnel stationed at the tops and crosstrees during a sail evolution both as safety observers and to assist with handling lines from aloft as needed.

topping lift. Purchase used for raising or taking the weight of a boom.

trick wheel. The emergency helm located on the fantail of *Eagle*.

"Trim." Adjust sails to take best advantage of the wind. Sheets, braces, and lifts are the lines normally adjusted when *trimming* sail.

truck. The top of a vessel's mast, as in the *main truck*.

true wind. The direction and speed at which the wind is actually blowing observed from a static frame of reference. In contrast, **relative wind** is based on the movements of the observer.

truss. A heavy swivel with a horizontal and vertical pivot forming the center of motion for bracing a yard.

turnbuckle. Rigging hardware at the base of shrouds, backstays, and forestays that is used to tension wire rope rigging to ensure masts are oriented correctly. Also known as *bottles*.

two-blocked. A purchase is two-blocked when the two blocks have been pulled as close together as possible.

tye. Part of the purchase used to raise the movable yards. On *Eagle* it consists of a chain made fast to the center of the yard. The chain is led up through a sheave in the mast down to a fly block through which the halyard purchase is rove.

unfurl. To cast loose a sail by throwing off the gaskets.

"Up behind." Drop the line so that it may be belayed quickly. This command is given to personnel behind the line captain and is used when belaying a line and enough turns are on the pin so that one person can hold it.

vang. A line leading from the mizzen gaff to the deck to keep it steady when the mizzensails are not set (used in pairs on *Eagle*).

veer. (1) In the Northern Hemisphere, a shift in the direction of the wind in a clockwise direction. Also called **haul**. (2) To pay out or let out a greater length of chain or rope; specifically, to veer chain when anchoring.

waist. The portion of the main weather deck between the raised forecastle deck and the poop deck.

"Walk away with." Grasp a line with both hands and walk away (move away) with it. Used when hauling on a line, usually a halyard.

waterway. The gutter on each side of a ship's deck that carries excess water to the scuppers.

wearing. The process of bringing the ship's stern through the wind to get the wind on the opposite side; same as jibing on a fore-and-aft rigged vessel.

"Wear-O." An information command issued by the officer of the deck that *Eagle* has begun a wearing evolution.

weather. On the side toward the wind. Objects on that side are referred to as *to windward* or *to weather.*

weather helm. A condition where lee rudder must be used in order to keep the vessel on a steady course. This is caused by more force aft of the pivot point forcing the bow to windward. Although excessive weather helm is undesirable, *Eagle* and most sailing vessels are designed to sail with some weather helm, especially when sailing **by the wind** (usually less than 10 degrees of rudder).

whip. A line or purchase used to lift or pull a load, such as on the cargo boom. Also known as a *hoist.*

winter housing. A special fitting on the front of the topmast cap band, used to store the topgallant yard when it is unshipped in the process of housing the topgallant mast.

worm, parcel, and serve. A method of protecting standing rigging. *Worming* is the process of filling the lays of a rope with small stuff wound spirally. *Parceling* consists of winding tarred canvas around a rope, while *serving* involves winding small stuff tightly around a rope to hold the worming and parceling in position. The direction to work can be remembered by using this phrase: "Worm and parcel with the lay, turn and serve the other way."

yard. A spar rigged horizontally on a mast, to which the head of a square sail is bent (made fast).

yardarm. Outboard end of a yard.

yoke. The U-shaped steel bar that is secured to the center of the yard and to the truss.

INDEX

The Naval Institute Press is the book-publishing arm of the U.S. Naval Institute, a private, nonprofit, membership society for sea service professionals and others who share an interest in naval and maritime affairs. Established in 1873 at the U.S. Naval Academy in Annapolis, Maryland, where its offices remain today, the Naval Institute has members worldwide.

Members of the Naval Institute support the education programs of the society and receive the influential monthly magazine *Proceedings* or the colorful bimonthly magazine *Naval History* and discounts on fine nautical prints and on ship and aircraft photos. They also have access to the transcripts of the Institute's Oral History Program and get discounted admission to any of the Institute-sponsored seminars offered around the country.

The Naval Institute's book-publishing program, begun in 1898 with basic guides to naval practices, has broadened its scope to include books of more general interest. Now the Naval Institute Press publishes about seventy titles each year, ranging from how-to books on boating and navigation to battle histories, biographies, ship and aircraft guides, and novels. Institute members receive significant discounts on the Press's more than eight hundred books in print.

Full-time students are eligible for special half-price membership rates. Life memberships are also available.

For a free catalog describing Naval Institute Press books currently available, and for further information about joining the U.S. Naval Institute, please write to:

Member Services
U.S. Naval Institute
291 Wood Road
Annapolis, MD 21402-5034
Telephone: (800) 233-8764
Fax: (410) 571-1703
Web address: www.usni.org